TO GLENDA

and

TO ALL THOSE PEOPLE WHO CONQUER LIFE'S CHALLENGES DESPITE ADVERSITY

ARCH OF FIRE

A CHILD IN NAZI GERMANY

Siegfried Streufert

**AINA
KAI
BOOKS**

ISBN 0-9644318-0-7
Library of Congress Catalog Card Number 94-73377
Copyright © 1993, 1995 by Siegfried Streufert
All Rights Reserved

Printed in the United States of America
Published in the German language under the title "Drachenwind"

CONTENTS

iv

PREFACE

This book tells of a childhood in the midst of Nazi persecution. It recounts the daily hail of allied bombs that rained down upon us then. It speaks of fears and horrors during the Nazi period, but it also speaks of love, of games, of the mischievousness of being a child - of a childhood anywhere, at any time. This book speaks of life despite the day-to-day events. It speaks of a time when adversity became normalcy - as it does for children and for all those who have never experienced a happier life.

My father had fought the Nazis before they took power in Germany. He continued to work against them within the underground movement. The Nazis never uncovered his clandestine activities, yet they continued to suspect us. We lived with persecution. We longed for the day the "Third Reich" might collapse, hoping to survive until that fateful day. Yet once the war was over, many Allied soldiers considered us to be nothing more than just another "bad German" family. Like everyone else, they thought, we must surely be partly responsible for all the misdeeds of Naziism, never considering that not **all** Germans had been Nazis.

But this book tells of more than what happened to our family. It tells of the German people at that time, of those who went along with the Nazis - and of those who fought them from within. It tells of individuals who knew and understood - and of those who did not. It tells of lives ruled by a particular totalitarian regime. Viewed from another perspective, it tells of people who could have lived in any totalitarian country, during any century of human existence.

Persecution, violence, and war occur again and again, all over the world. This terrible cycle has persisted across centuries. People persecute other people. Sometimes the discrimination is subtle, at other times it is violent to the point of genocide. The twentieth century, supposedly marked by ethics and advanced civilization, has not been an exception. Think, for example, of the killing of native Indians in the Amazon. Think of Soviet persecution of anyone who did not quite "fit" with the views of the regime...the callous murder of eleven million people by the Nazi movement...the "ethnic cleansing" in former Yugoslavia. It continues while we watch - and turn away. After all, it is not happening to us. True, we care a little, enough to condemn those horrible acts. But our outrage and our response to mass murder are not sufficient to discourage those who perpetrate those crimes. And, by our inaction, we may just encourage others who believe that they can initiate their own campaign of persecution and suppression with immunity.

Of course, we believe that it cannot happen "here," wherever our own "here" might be. But can we be sure? Often, suppression begins quite subtly, possibly with just a few prejudicial statements condemning some "scapegoat" segment of the population. After a while, few doubt the validity of that propaganda. People no longer object to actions that follow; after all, those actions seem to be justified. And people who are not (or not yet) persecuted simply shrug off those actions as exceptions to the rule, as irrelevant to their own personal pursuit of happiness. After all, they want to go on with their own lives.

The Reverend Martin Niemöller, a prominent German Protestant theologian during the Nazi period said later: "When the Nazis arrested the Communists, I said nothing; after all, I wasn't a Communist. When they locked up the Social Democrats, I was silent; I wasn't a Social Democrat. When they picked up the Catholics, I did not protest, after all, I was not Catholic. And by the time they arrested me, there was nobody left who could have objected." Unfortunately, people learn to look the other way, to accept the horror that is perpetrated upon others.

We can even learn to accept our own suffering. It is a tragedy that horror can begin to seem like "normalcy." Most people simply learn to live with it. We can live with cancer. We can live with bombs or artillery shells falling upon us day and night. We can live with death and destruction around us. We want to go on living. We protect ourselves as well as we can. And, if it appears useful, we learn to ignore the pain of our neighbors. We refuse to help others whenever that help might endanger our own lives....

Some among us will even profit from the suffering of our

vii

fellow man. Think of Nazi industrial managers who willingly utilized forced labor. Think of the story about "King Rat," of the American who took advantage of fellow prisoners of war (a book by James Clavell).

Others among us will simply succumb to authority. We will do what we are told to do no matter how horrible those actions might be. Sometimes we follow orders because a refusal would threaten our own lives or the lives of those we love. At other times, people follow orders simply because the person giving the order is an "authority."

Stanley Milgram performed an experiment with normal American college students. They were told that they would function as "teachers" and were introduced to another student who would be the "learner." Whenever the learner would fail to answer a question correctly, the "teacher" student was to administer an electric shock to the learner. And whenever the learner would again fail to respond accurately, an authority figure told the "teacher" to turn up the level of the electric shock.

At 75 volts, the learner (who, unknown to the "teacher," was not actually shocked) would grunt. At 120 Volts there would be loud complaints. At 225 volts agonized screams were heard. And once the dial read 330 Volts, the learner fell silent, apparently unconscious or possibly even dead. Yet over 60% of the college student "teachers," when ordered to do so by an older "authority" person in a white lab coat, turned up the electric shock level again and again until the label on the shock generator read 450 Volts! More than sixty percent of perfectly normal American college students were obeying orders to harm - possibly even kill - another person, even though many among them expressed concerns about the welfare of their victim!

Of course, we may take solace in the fact that more than 30% refused to accept the order. But how many among those 30% would have gone along if their own lives had depended on obedience? Surely, a few courageous ones might have objected. A few brave, ethical persons exist in every country, in every century. In Germany, they were the few who joined the underground movement. Most of them died fighting the Nazis from within the country. In America, they were the few who objected when Americans of Japanese descent were shipped off to concentration camps. In Russia, they were killed or sent to labor camps in Siberia when they protested Stalin's inhumane deeds. Today, those courageous few are the men and women who stand up to the Moamar Kadaffis and Sadam Husseins of our time.

While a few among us are fighting for freedom and justice, and while the many accept whatever happens, life continues. For the persecuted, it is a strange and often horrendous life. For those who are not (yet) persecuted, it is merely changed normalcy. Life does go on. It is human nature to accept things as they are: If we cannot accept life as it is, our chances of survival are diminished.

As a child, I had no choice but to accept whatever life would bring - both the good and the horrible. It was all I knew. I had not experienced a different, a better world that I could have compared to day-to-day events of my life then. The love of my parents, the little pleasures of day-to-day experiences and the company of my friend sustained me. But I could never be certain, as most children in most places are, that life would continue. I had to live in constant fear of the Nazis. I was terrified by the Allied bombs that, piece by piece, demolished our town. As evening fell, I would never know whether I would live to see the next day's sunrise....

Some among us survived. Others lost their lives. I lived to remember - and I lived to write the tales that follow. I lived to tell what it was like to be a child in Nazi Germany.

A NOTE TO THE READER

The events described in these tales are exactly what I remember. Some readers have asked whether I might not have introduced the thoughts of the adult I am today into the experiences, the feelings, and the words of the child I once was. I am sure that I did not.

The events of my childhood, of Nazi persecution, of day and night air attacks, did not make for pleasant memories. For decades, I would not think about those times. For decades, I had blocked out every memory of those experiences. Then, two years ago, the mayor of the town where I grew up met with me. He was writing a book about my father (which has since appeared: <u>Aktion Gitter</u>, Ostsee Verlag, D 24221, Raisdorf, Germany). He needed pictures and documents. As I looked at pictures and pored over documents for his use, memories of that time crept hauntingly into my consciousness. They returned unadulterated by intervening experiences. I started to write this book immediately after looking at the pictures, after reading my father's letters and my mother's notes. I felt, once again, all the things that I had felt at that time, about fifty years ago. It all came back, just as it had been then. To my own surprise, the thoughts, the words, the sentences of that childhood were recaptured as I began to write what I had spoken then.

THE EARLY WAR YEARS

THE SEARCH

It was a Sunday in early June 1939, about twenty minutes before ten in the morning.

My parents liked to linger in bed on Sundays. They talked, even sang a song together before getting up and making breakfast. After all, Sundays were different from weekdays. With all the work that my father had to do, with all the traveling, and all the help my mother gave him - all that she did in addition to taking care of the house and raising me, they deserved some morning peace and quiet. And I was quite happy about those late Sunday mornings. Our radio played classical music until eleven; I liked that music. Probably my father would rather have heard operettas, but it did not matter: He was occupied in their bedroom. So I enjoyed these mornings.

On this occasion, a finch sang in the quince tree outside of my window. I imagined the bird appreciated my music and was singing along. The window was wide open and fresh spring air was gently moving the lace window curtains back and forth.

Finally, I heard my parents getting up. They were beginning to make breakfast together. On Sundays, I was allowed to come to breakfast in a robe. I still had time. I decided not to join them right away - I did not yet want to interrupt that warm, pleasant, sunny feeling. So I stayed in bed.

Suddenly, there was a harsh pounding on the front door. The doorbell rang insistently at the same time.

My mother opened the door. Three men pushed her out of the way and forced themselves into our hallway. Even though I was only wearing a nightshirt, I ran to see what was happening. A five year old runs around without being fully dressed - it doesn't matter.

I knew one of those three men: the local policeman. He seemed just a bit embarrassed. From time to time we had spoken a few words with him, always on the street outside, nothing important. But we lived in a town of only eight hundred people, and we knew about all of the inhabitants of the town, more or less.

The second intruder also seemed a bit familiar. But I was

2

not sure. Maybe all of those who wore brown Nazi shirts and black boots looked the same. But the third one - I knew I had never seen him before. He was wearing a suit, and he stared at me with angry, unpleasant eyes. "We are going to search the house!" he barked at nobody in particular. Somehow he looked and acted as though he was more important than the other two. He opened all the doors leading from the hallway to other rooms, I guess to orient himself. "Where is the basement?"

My father had finished dressing and emerged from the bedroom. "Can I help you?" he asked in a tone of voice I had not heard before. "What are you doing here on a Sunday morning?"

"We are going to search your house!" the important one barked again. He reminded me of that angry hound a neighbor kept tied up in the yard. One day that dog had torn off a piece of my playmate's ear. This man would do something like that!

He stared at my father. Now he sounded sarcastic: "We are going to get you!" His hand moved horizontally across his neck as though he was cutting off his own head. A triumphant look crept over his face.

They started searching. Books were flying off our shelves. They found nothing behind those books except bare walls. Nothing behind the cabinets in the study except a little dust. The drawers were ripped out of my father's desk - I would have been afraid to pull them out gently! I would never have touched the contents of those drawers! But these three were not bothered by anything!

They found only supplies and some papers related to my father's work, nothing that was of interest to them. Next they marched into my bedroom. The bed had not yet been made and the radio was still playing.

The man in the suit looked suspiciously at the radio. "That is a big radio," he said. "You can listen to foreign stations with that thing. You know that is forbidden. You must trade it for a People's Radio, one that receives only German stations!" He looked expectantly at my father, but there was no response.

So he and the other two continued to search. But our local policeman only made believe that he was searching for things. I don't think he was paying attention to anything he was touching. He seemed terribly uncomfortable.

I would have loved to know what they were looking for... If I had known, I would have hurried to hide it better, very quickly. But I was too young to know all the things that were or were not allowed during the Nazi years.

I watched the three men - from some distance, of course. It seemed so strange that they would just push themselves into the house - that they would throw everything around. I did not like it. Well, I thought, sometimes grown-ups are hard to understand. They don't make sense. These people did not even let us eat our breakfast! And I was getting hungry. At that moment it did not occur to me that they could find something "illegal" - and that the consequences could be terrible.

But, then, I remembered a few books on the shelf. The dust covers had been changed. The books inside were forbidden. The covers outside were taken from books that were allowed. It was curious, the Nazis had searched our house several times. They had just been through the book shelves all over again, yet they never thought that the books might be different than their jackets. "They must be pretty stupid," I thought.

I was vaguely aware that there would be other things, hidden things, that were illegal too. But I was too young to know exactly what those things might be, and I certainly did not know where they might be hidden.

The one object that I knew could displease them was that sad picture in the hallway. It was a lithograph, an old painting that had recently become a protest picture against Hitler. Actually, I had never liked the picture: it was too sad. An old woman was sitting on a park bench, in Vienna I think, crying bitterly. Her husband had put his arm around her shoulders and was staring into the distance. He didn't look happy either. He did not try to comfort her. The whole scene was so unpleasant!

Just the previous week, I had asked my mother about the picture. "Why do we have to have such a sad picture?"

"Those are people who used to live in South Tirol. At the end of the World War, southern Tirol was given to the Italians. And now Hitler has finally given their home away forever, because he wants Mussolini to be his friend. Now the old woman and that old man are sitting in a park in Vienna. They don't have a home anymore."

I could understand why those two would be sad. If someone had chased me away from my home town, I would have been unhappy too.

"But, don't tell the story of that picture to anyone," my mother reminded me, "we are not supposed to have such a picture." I got the message. I had learned long ago that anything we would say at home was not to be repeated anywhere else.

The three men had been in the basement. They had inspected our supply of coal, whatever was left from heating the house in the winter. They had looked at canned foods. They came back upstairs. The entire house was an unbelievable mess. I was not the most orderly child in the world, but this kind of mess was awful, even for me. Sure, my mother had to remind me from time to time to put away my toys. But in comparison to those three, I was extremely good about cleaning up!

The angry man in the suit had come into the kitchen and moved very close to my mother, nearly pushing her into the wall. His eyes were hard, yet mocking. "Where are you hiding everything?" he wanted to know.

"What are you looking for?"

Now he yelled; "You know perfectly well what we are looking for! Don't pretend innocence!"

"Nearly like Kafka" she mentioned under her breath as he turned away.

"Nearly like what?" he screamed. I guess he had never heard of Kafka. As a five year old, I had not heard of him either. The civilian's face had turned bright red. He looked intently at the walls in the room. His eyes stopped when he saw the sad picture through the open kitchen door. I was scared and started to tremble a little. I had a funny feeling in my stomach.

"What kind of picture is that?" he demanded.

"A lithograph."

"I know that!" He seemed in thought for a minute. "That is such nonsense," he continued with sharp anger in his voice. "We are living in Germany's finest hour. Our armies will

5

conquer the world. Adolf Hitler has made all that possible. This is a glorious time. His picture should hang there, not such sad nonsense! If you had the sense to hang up a beautiful picture of Adolf Hitler, instead of that kind of garbage, we probably would not have to search your house! But that is something you will probably never learn!"

He turned and the other two followed him. As he opened the front door on the way out, he looked back: "Next time we will surely get you! Then you've all had it! Heil Hitler!"

They were gone. My parents looked at each other, with much love, yet very somberly. I pushed myself closer to my mother. Somehow I was still afraid. And still hungry. That comment about the picture, that it is much too sad..., I thought he was right about that. But everything else they had said and done.....

WAR

It was September 1939. I was sitting by the window, from time to time looking at the book on my lap, at other times listening to my parents' conversation. They were talking about war.

"What is war?" I wanted to know. My father looked at me for a while. "When people make war, they want to take things that belong to people in another country."

It reminded me of the older kid I had been playing with on a sand pile outside. He had tried to keep my toy car. Just thinking of it made me angry. "They shouldn't take things that belong to other people. They should stop it!"

My mother smiled. She would never have taken anything that belonged to someone else. Quite the opposite; she was always giving things away. Then I remembered the older boy, last week, who hit me when I did not do what he wanted. I asked, "When they have a war, do they hurt the other people?"

"Yes, they even kill them." My father's face was very serious. He had been a soldier during the First World War.

"That is ugly!" I could not quite understand why people would want to kill others. "Can't someone stop it?"

My father responded. "Once wars start, they usually go on for a long time." He creased his forehead but smiled at me at the same time. But his large steel-blue eyes remained a bit distant. "Sometimes for many years...."

"Will the war come here?"

This time my mother answered. She looked directly at me, with love and warmth in her brown eyes: "Maybe God will protect us from the war."

I thought about her answer. We had not spoken much about God. "Mommy," I said, "how do people know that there is a God?"

She smiled: "Look, Siegfried, human beings did not make all the big mountains and the lakes and the trees and all the animals. So there must be something that is able to make all those things!"

Certainly, I could not have made the mountains. Maybe

a small one in the sandpile near the house, but not big ones, like those in my picture book of the Alps. And I did not know any other people who could build mountains or lakes. They could plant a tree, but that was not the same as "making" one.

"But, mommy, how do we know that it has the name 'God'?"

She smiled again. "Sweetheart, it doesn't make any difference what we call it. We call it God because it does so many good things. Other people in other countries have a different name for it. It lets everything around us grow so that we have enough to eat. It lets us live and lets us be healthy. So we call it our God."

"Well," I thought "if it is a nice God, then it probably will not let the war come here." It was a comforting thought.

SCHOOL

Half a year had passed. I was not quite six years old. First grade was waiting. My parents had kept me out of kindergarten. They knew that the teacher was a Nazi. But first grade was compulsory. They had no choice.

Our local grade school was small: There were only three class rooms - one of them was used to store old furniture. Children from the first four grades all sat together in the same room. Some lessons were in common for all of us; in other subjects, the teacher would only talk to one of the grades. All the rest of the kids were supposed to do assigned work at that time.

My best friend Friedrich-Karl and I always sat together. I liked that. We could whisper to each other, and later, after we had learned to write, we would scribble notes to each other.

Our first grade teacher was a Mr. Kerner. I liked him. He was friendly. He told funny stories. It was fun to learn. But he did not last long. He was drafted and, only a few days later, the news came that he had been killed in action. We heard a rumor that his death in combat was not true. A couple of weeks earlier, Mr. Kerner supposedly made some comment that was not favorable toward the Nazi government. According to the rumor, his draft and "death in combat" had been "arranged." We never found out whether the rumor was correct.

We got another teacher. At first, that new teacher seemed to like me. I grasped the material quickly and was mostly interested in things he said. Most of the time, my grades were A's with a few B's. Even in "Behavior" I earned an A. It was surprising, in a way, since this teacher had told us "God deserves an A, Hitler deserves a B, and children cannot expect more than a C in anything!"

But I did not like this man. He was not as nice as Mr. Kerner. He clearly had favorites among the kids and seemed to dislike others. Klaus and Maria, twin children of a laborer, were always in trouble. Who knows what those two kids were fed at home; they frequently had indigestion. As a consequence, they did not smell very pleasantly! Some other child sitting nearby

9

would gleefully announce the odor to the teacher: "Something stinks like sulfur!"

That would bring a delighted smile to the teacher's face. He would walk directly toward Klaus and Maria. They were ordered to stand up; the teacher would bend down to suck in the air back of them. We could hear his nose snorting. "Both of you again!" he would yell loudly. His voice seemed full of disgust, yet delight.

He would instruct the two children to come to the front of the classroom, making sure that all of us could watch their punishment. With a haughty smile on his face, he would get his bamboo stick, bend it back and forth a bit, tap it on the floor to test it. Then he would demand that the two kids bend over - each would receive ten harsh hits on their buttocks. But neither of them would ever cry. They were accustomed to the pain. It had happened much too often.

The same punishment would be meted out to all who had not done their homework and to those who were unable to answer the teacher's questions. One older kid who had never advanced beyond the first grade, even though he was already about fourteen years old, was beaten daily. He was retarded and could not answer the teacher's questions. Who knows whether he even understood what the teacher was asking!

Friedrich-Karl and I never had such problems. All in all, there were about four children in first grade who were intelligent enough to satisfy this teacher. But, we still had our problems with him.

One day, during the break between classes, we were playing outside. I saw the teacher coming from the building, carrying a very large and very hard medicine ball. He asked a few of the kids to catch it. None of us first graders was able to hold onto the ball; it was much too heavy. At one point, the teacher turned to me. He threw the ball at me with full force. It hit me in the stomach. I fell, gasping for air. The teacher laughed with great amusement and, with sarcasm in his voice, mocked, "And you want to become a German soldier?"

Once I was able to breathe again I answered. "No I don't. I don't want to be a soldier!"

That was the end. Whatever positive feelings he might have had towards me were gone. And as long as he was our teacher, there were no more "A" grades in "Behavior."

Not much later, all of us the kids were again playing outside. We used a soccer ball, throwing and kicking it from kid to kid. Some of us yelled and screamed; it was all part of the game. Suddenly the teacher came storming out of the building. "Shut up," he yelled even louder than we had been screaming. "You are acting like little Jews! This is not a Jew School!"

That evening, I told my father. His face became very hard. His large steel-blue eyes stared beyond me, seemingly far into the past. Finally he spoke, not in a loud voice, but with anger. "That kind of thing is a great injustice. My best buddy in the last war was Jewish. He fought just as hard for Germany as I did. He was wounded on the same day as I. He was and is a German. He loved Germany. It is unjust that our country no longer returns that love. A teacher who does not understand that is incompetent."

He was quiet and seemed deep in thought for a while. And then he turned towards me and spoke more gently. "But you know that you can't repeat that in school."

I knew.

ATTACK

November 1940. The sirens had sent their wails across town on many nights before. Alarm! Hostile aircraft above! We had heard the anti-aircraft guns fire again and again at the phantom planes in the sky. One of the gun positions was not far from us, hidden in a forest known as "Birdsong." This gun was especially loud, probably because it was closer to us than the others. I used to call it "Dun-Cluck." That is how it sounded.

Initially we did not take all that noise very seriously. We were sure that the planes were heading somewhere else - maybe to bomb Berlin, or some other important city. Probably they were just passing by. And if they should decide to attack downtown Kiel, the nearby city, the bombs would fall far from us. After all, our house was in a small town, a suburb, about ten long kilometers from the city center of Kiel.

One evening the shooting started somewhere around eight thirty. I was already in bed - the racket did not bother me very much. At about ten o'clock everything was quiet again and I fell asleep. My parents had gone to bed too. They were tired and, I am sure, they too were soon asleep.

Later on, all of us were awakened again. We heard the firing of distant anti-aircraft guns. The noise was coming closer. Finally, all the anti-aircraft batteries around us joined in. It was a hellish concert. A few minutes later, we heard another sound, a humming, getting louder and louder: the sound of many propellers.

Then, suddenly, a howl and shrill whistling. A horrendous noise followed. The house shook as though it was frightened. Glass was flying around my bed. For a second I was lying still, as if paralyzed, incredibly shocked and scared. Then I jumped up and ran toward my parents' bedroom. My feet were cut by glass on the floor.

"What is that light?"

Bright daylight in the middle of the night! But it was a strange light, somewhere between yellow and red.

"Fire!"

My mother grabbed me. The light shone from the

direction of the entrance to the house. But our house was not burning. Not this time. The strange light entered through the glass of our outside door. We ran to look.

It was a terrifying picture. Hundreds of incendiary bombs had eerily brightened the evening fog. The misty air had turned orange-red, but around all those places where bombs were burning, the light was bright yellow. It looked like the end of the world. I could not understand what I was seeing. I was so frightened by all that strange light! I pressed myself closer to my mother and covered my eyes with my hands: "Make it go away, please!"

My father searched the house from attic to basement. He wanted to make sure that none of the bombs had hit our house. There were none. We had been lucky - this time. Only some of the windows had been shattered. My mother put antiseptic on my cut feet and bandaged them.

We quickly dressed. I had calmed down a bit. We went outside to see what had happened. Incendiary bombs were lying everywhere: on the street, in front yards, on the meadows around us. The second and third houses up the street were on fire. Another house suddenly burst into flames. It began to rain, with a little snow mixed in. The rain helped the local fire department to put out most of the fires, but not until the entire roof and the top floor of a neighbor's home were gone.

A number of other houses had been badly damaged by the terrifying bombs that we had heard howling and whistling down from the sky. Roof shingles were gone, windows were shattered, walls had collapsed. It was incomprehensible. Night had turned into a strange red and yellow day. The familiar town, my home town, was strangely transformed into fire and, in some places, into rubble. I looked, I wanted to see, but I was afraid to look. All those colors were interesting, and, in a strange sort of way, even fascinating - but so ugly!

After a while, all the fires were out. It was still raining. We went back home, to a house with shattered windows. My parents covered the gaping holes with blankets and cardboard to keep out the rain and the cold.

"Why is this happening?" I wanted to know.

13

"That's what war is like," someone answered.

"Will it happen again? I don't want it to ever happen again!"

My mother took me into her arms to comfort me. "Maybe. Maybe it will happen again. But as long as all of us are together...." she hesitated. "I love you, but it is time to go to sleep now."

In the past, I had not been afraid to go to sleep. The noise of the anti-aircraft guns had been strange, but it had also been somehow amusing. Especially that Dun-Cluck gun. Now it was all very different. In the evenings, I no longer wanted to go to bed.

"We can't go to sleep, the planes are going to come." I would say. Every time I closed my eyes, I would see the yellow and red fires, the incendiary bombs. I would try very hard to keep my eyes open so I would not see that ugly, pretty light.

"Let's go down to the basement right now!" I pleaded. "Maybe the bombs can't touch us there. I know they are coming again tonight!" My parents tried to calm me as well as they could. But somehow I knew that they themselves did not feel calm, no matter how hard they tried to comfort me. And this horrible night was only the first of many more air attacks to come. Bombs would fall more and more frequently. I was afraid for weeks, for months, and to some extent even for years. But slowly, very slowly, the fear began to abate. When one experiences horror again and again, its impact diminishes, even if it is the terror of bombs.

WHAT IS IN A NAME?

One day the teacher asked me whether I understood the meaning of my own name. "What does it mean to have a name like Siegfried?" he demanded. He had a son, younger than I, born while the Nazis had already been in power for a year or two. His son was the only other "Siegfried" in town. If one separates the name Siegfried into its two syllables, "Sieg" means victory and "Fried(en)" means peace. I responded with the interpretation I had heard from my parents: "The name means 'Victory for Peace; peace shall be victorious.' We don't want war!"

The teacher was annoyed. "No!" he answered emphatically. "You don't know what you are talking about. Who told you such nonsense? Siegfried means: first we have to be victorious, then we will have peace!"

His answer did not fit my image of the "Siegfried" hero in the ancient Nibelungen Saga. Siegfried was always helping others. On my last birthday, my parents had given me a thin book with a child's version of the old saga. It told about that mythical time. By now I was able to read quite well and had read that little book more than once. Sometimes I even persuaded my mother to read those old stories to me.

Yes conflict and fighting was part of the Nibelungen tales. But the "good guys" subdued the "bad guys." It meant preventing the villains from killing and doing harm. I understood that, on some rare occasions, it might be necessary to force people to live in peace. Just like on the playground: sometimes adults had to stop little kids from fighting. And sometimes they did have to use some force to do that. But to fight with another person, or against another country, just to conquer - that did not fit my view of a "fair" world. To me, "Siegfried" meant what I saw in the Nibelungen Saga: a representation of things that are good, a representation of light rather than darkness.

True, the "good" and the "light" would, at times, be replaced by the "bad" and the "darkness." Occasionally, the bad guys would win. But, in turn, darkness had to give way to goodness and light. Night would follow day, but day would follow night. The Nazis were the bad guys; they were making war. But, just as in the Nibelungen Saga, they would not last forever. Some day our world would be peaceful again.

Today we know that he "final victory" for the Nazis, something this teacher surely anticipated, was not to be. The Nazis lost their war - and Germany lost much more than just a war. Even so, there was a different kind of victory: the victory of peace, at least for a while, and at least for Europe. And even this teacher - I don't know whether by necessity or through insight - changed his views as the "Third Reich" collapsed into ashes. I have wondered how he interpreted the meaning of his son's name in those later years.

SLAPPING THE FÜHRER

It was one of those cool, rainy days that are not at all infrequent in Schleswig-Holstein, the narrow lands between the North Sea and the Baltic. My mother was sitting in the living room, mending some of my father's clothes. Every week the stores were emptier. Old, worn out clothes could no longer be thrown out - they had to be repaired again and again until the material became so thin that it ripped at the slightest touch. I was sitting on the floor. Somewhere I had obtained a wooden box, maybe two feet square. The cover was gone but the other five sides were painted a lovely red. I liked that box. Once it served as a container for my building blocks, then one day I had thought of a better use for it. I asked my father to drill a small hole precisely in the center of the bottom. I pushed a small bolt through the bottom and attached narrow strips of metal to the bolt. One of the strips was inside the box, the other outside. Their location had to match exactly: I was building a radio.

I wrote the names of radio stations on both sides: Berlin. London. Hamburg. Copenhagen. Stockholm. Setting the box on its side, I made sure that the metal strip would point to the same stations on each of the two sides. And I made sure that one could turn the strips from station to station. Now I was ready to play a game. "Mommy, could you change the station on my radio from time to time? I will be each station!" I put my head inside the box and announced the station name whenever my mother turned the dial. I would hum or sing a song, play my harmonica or even get my father's zither to make music as well as I could. It was fun! From time to time, I left my box to remind my mother to switch stations. After all, it was difficult to be the same station for a long period of time.

At one point I decided to broadcast the news. Among other information, I repeated an item I had heard on our real radio the previous day. "A German submarine sank a British passenger ship not far from the English Coast."

I crawled out of my radio box and looked at my mother: "Why did they do that?"

"In a war, people destroy anything another country has!"

"I know. But if it was a passenger ship, there must have been people on it. Mothers and children, just like the two of us. We have nothing to do with the war!"

"In war, nobody cares who gets hurt and who doesn't. Besides, Hitler probably wanted them to do that."

"I don't like him!" I thought for a while. Then I had an idea. "Mommy, in the Nibelungen Saga, Siegfried has a cap. When he wears it, nobody can see him. I think it is probably just a story, but could there be such a thing?"

"No, that kind of cap does not exist. If it did, would you want one?"

"It would be great!"

"But what would you do with it?"

"I would go to Berlin or to any place where Hitler is. And every time he does something stupid, I would slap his face. Real hard. He wouldn't know where the slap came from. I would step back fast, so he could not touch me. He would grab the air, but he could not find me! It would be so funny! And I would hit him again if he did something else that would hurt people. Maybe then he would stop the war and all the other nasty things he does!"

My mother smiled at me. "Too bad that there is no such thing!"

THE CRASH

This time, the sirens screamed at about eleven at night. Air attack! We turned on the radio; its antenna was attached to the phone line. Information about the location of enemy planes was broadcast via the telephone system to make sure that attacking aircraft could not locate the broadcast source. Between announcements, the station would tick like an alarm clock. It was ticking now. Then, a matter-of-fact, distant voice announced that "enemy planes" were heading directly for us. Take cover!

"Looks like we are going to get it again," my mother commented in a quiet voice. She was just lifting a hanger with a coat off the rod in our hall closet. She turned the hanger around. All hangers had to face in the same direction: with the closed part outward, toward us. That way we could grasp a whole bunch of clothes at once in case the bombs would set our house on fire tonight.

We had already been hit by a number of incendiary bombs. My father had been able to extinguish the fires very quickly. Earlier incendiary bombs were not filled with phosphorous. Water would put out the flames. We had buckets of water and bags of sand standing everywhere.

Later incendiary bombs would become much more of a problem because many of them contained phosphorus. You could tell these canisters apart from "normal" ones: phosphorous canisters had an extra red stripe. They could not be extinguished with water. Fortunately, so far our house had been hit only with "normal" bombs. We had thought about what action we might take if a phosphorus fire had started. We could pick the canister up with a shovel and throw it out through a window - but only if we had found it quickly enough. We knew people who had not been fast enough to save their homes. After all, it was very dangerous to search the house while explosive bombs were still hurling down. You had to wait for a lull in the air attack. During a lull, people would quickly leave the basement to check for fires upstairs. Nonetheless, quite a few people had been killed as they tried to put out the fires upstairs - just as the bombs started falling again.

The anti-aircraft battery in the "Birdsong Forest" started its concert; a clear sign that the "Tommys" or the "Angels," as we called the British planes, were now above us. It was always the British who came at night. Once America entered the war, we were often under attack twice during the same twenty-four hours. But the "Ammys," the American planes, seemed to prefer daytime.

Our neighbors across the street did not have a basement. There was no way they could hide from the bombs. Consequently, they became our frequent nighttime companions. Not that our basement was truly safe, but it was better than nothing. Each time when nearby anti-aircraft guns joined the hellish chorus, they came running to join us.

The humming of many motors was getting louder and louder. British and American planes would hum, German planes would buzz. Humming meant bombs and fires and rubble. Searchlights drilled their beams through the night sky, moving slowly back and forth, searching and searching - waiting to spot a sacrificial airplane.

We were standing at the front door, looking upwards. We gained an advantage by watching diligently. The British were incredibly reliable! Someone, probably somewhere in London, would decide which part of our city was to be leveled each day. The planes could identify those thirty or forty square blocks, even in bad weather - or so we believed. But to make absolutely sure that exactly the intended apartments would be destroyed, the planes would carefully mark the area. First, they would drop "christmas trees," bright lights suspended from parachutes that would slowly drift downward, illuminating everything below. The lights were dropped in groups, like christmas decorations in the sky. Step by step, the planes would light more and more of those "trees." Then colored markers fell to the ground, locating the intended "ground zero."

Today we were probably lucky! They had decided to destroy part of the bedroom community "Elmschenhagen," the next suburb to our west.

The whistling and howling of the bombs screamed through the night, not as loud as yesterday. The thumping sound of explosions followed. Flashes of the many detonations exploded about two miles away.

We stayed at the front door. High clouds above Elmschenhagen turned yellowish-red, reflecting the burning houses and apartments below. We continued to watch. If it were not so horrible, those lights - those flickering flames in the distance, all the christmas trees above - might have been beautiful fireworks. But we knew all too well what they meant. We had experienced the horror ourselves, over and over again. This "beauty" was so ugly, so appalling!

Now a search light had captured a British airplane. Three or four other searchlights joined it, criss-crossing the target. The lights were adamant: they did not want to lose that "Angel." The anti-aircraft batteries started firing toward the place where the lights met. Points of color moved upwards toward that plane. The pilot tried dramatic escape maneuvers. For a split second they lost him, but soon the lights recaptured that little cross in the sky. More and more points of light moved toward the plane, exploding nearby. They kept missing their target. More anti-aircraft fire. Still the plane was there. Another anti-aircraft battery joined in. Now! The plane was burning! Everyone stared at it.

Anke, the sixteen year old daughter of our neighbor, was standing next to us. She was a pretty girl who was very much in love with a German soldier fighting somewhere deep in Russia. Would he survive? She cried when his letters did not arrive often enough.

Anke kept looking at the burning plane and at the trail of smoke that was clearly visible in one of the search lights. Slowly a smile crept over her pretty face. And then, as the plane suddenly began to fall, she danced excitedly up and down. "We killed one, we killed one!"

My mother turned toward her, very slowly. Her voice was grave. "He has a girlfriend somewhere, too."

Anke suddenly stood still. Her eyes froze over. Her mouth, which had just rejoiced in the words "We killed one," remained open, but now it seemed open in shock. Anke slowly turned and sat down on one of the steps.

Nobody spoke. The howling and thumping of the bombs continued.

FRIEDEL

My parents called me by a nickname, "Friedel." Of course, their love and desire for peace had persuaded them to give me the name Siegfried, the same impulse led them to shorten my name to its "peace" component.

But I did not like the nickname. Peace had nothing to do with it. "Friedel" could also be a girl's name! I liked girls. In fact, I always liked them more than boys - with the exception of my friend Friedrich-Karl, of course. But I was a boy. I wanted to be a boy. "Friedel" just did not fit.

Of course, other kids heard my parents use that nickname and started to use it too. How could I stop them? How could I make them call me by my real name? I wanted to be Siegfried, nothing else.

So every time some kid would call me "Friedel," I would, in a very official voice, announce that it was fine for him or her to use that name. However, there would be a charge of five Pfennig every time they called me Friedel, the money to be collected immediately. On the other hand, the name Siegfried would be free of charge.

Of course I had no way to enforce my rule. In fact, I never collected even one Pfennig. But somehow, the other kids must have believed my story. Soon nobody except, of course, my parents would call me "Friedel." It was a small victory - but to a child of six or seven it was an important one.

THE FROG'S LEG

There were quite a few kids in our suburb, but I hardly played with most of them. Somehow things did not work out when I tried. I well remember one incident that quickly ended my interest in a potential playmate.

Achim lived practically across the street from us. His father maintained the gardens and fields that belonged to the Rosenheim Restaurant. Next to the restaurant's garage was a small "servants' quarters" apartment. It was the home of Achim's family.

One day, I was working in "my" garden. Both of my parents were enthusiastic gardeners who were always encouraging me to follow their example. Their efforts had little success. Their garden was well known for many beautiful flowers, for the great strawberries they raised, and for much more. My little corner of the garden sprouted a wide variety of weeds. I had been reminded once again that my piece of ground needed to be weeded. There I sat, occasionally pulling up a weed, but mostly eating a mixture of strawberries and shelled peas from a large rhubarb leaf. Achim saw me from the street and yelled: "Want to come and play?"

I walked to the fence and told him that I had been told to clean up my own piece of garden before I could do anything else. He offered to help. I immediately accepted.

Neither one of us pulled out weeds. As we sat and talked about games we liked to play, a big frog jumped out of my weeds. Achim caught it in his hand: "He is not going to get away!"

"Why don't you let it go!?"

Achim vehemently shook his head. He held the little creature even tighter. "I don't like frogs! They are bad. They are good for nothing!"

"But that's not true! They eat mosquitos that bite us!"

"Not this one. It is not going to eat any more mosquitos." He opened his clenched hand. The frog dropped to the ground. One hind leg had been ripped from the animal's body. The creature could hardly move. "You did it!" Achim yelled at

24

me. "You hurt him!"

I protested. I had not even touched the frog! But Achim kept yelling. My parents came to see what was going on. Achim pointed his finger at me. "He pulled the leg off that frog!"

My father was instantly furious. He grabbed me and hit me. I was shocked, scared and horrified, all at once! Neither of my parents had ever hit me before! And I had not even done anything!

My mother tried to intervene. - But my father was not paying any attention to her. He only saw the mutilated animal. He was angry!

Achim was sent home. I cried a little. I did not want to cry: - more than anything I tried to tell them that I had not hurt that frog. I had not done it!

My mother took me into her arms. I stopped crying and looked at the two of them, upset that they would think I could hurt someone or something. I said it over and over again, slowly and firmly. Probably I did not sound like a child at that moment. "I did not do it. Achim had the frog in his hand. I never even touched it. Please don't think that I would ever do anything like that!"

I felt desperate. I wanted them to believe me. After all, I was telling the truth! Most of all, how could they believe I would do anything so horrible?!

I don't know whether they believed me. My father looked confused. My mother was crying, as though it was she who had been hit. But neither of them spoke. So I said it again and again: "I did not do it! I would never do anything like that...."

KITE-WIND

It was already late autumn. Some leaves still clung to the oak trees, but their green had turned to dark brown. The silver beeches, which held the clear majority in the nearby forest, had lost most of their leaves some weeks ago. But it was not yet quite as cold as it would soon be. Yesterday, a warm southerly wind had brought dreary rain. Today the sun was shining. Only a few grey clouds were chasing each other across the sky.

We had climbed out of bed quite early. I could just barely see a redness at the horizon - the glowing color that promised another day.

"Morning red pours rain into the pond." My father was studying the sunrise. I wanted to know what that sentence meant. "If the morning sky is red like this, it will probably rain very soon. In the evening it is different. Evening red means sunshine tomorrow." His eyes followed the sea gulls that seemed to be fleeing the coast this early morning. "And it will probably storm too." I was no longer sure he was talking to me.

During breakfast, my parents had been speaking quietly with each other. Now my father suddenly turned towards me and asked whether we should go and fly a kite. "It is good weather for a kite," he smiled. "With the wind outside, a kite should climb very nicely!"

It was a wonderful suggestion, but it made me sad. "We don't have a kite." I nearly cried. I thought about the fun we could have had - if we only had a kite!

My dad nearly laughed and calmed my unhappiness. "We can build one!"

Prior to the First World War my father had learned to be a master cabinet maker. During that war, a shell fragment pierced his chest. His lungs were seriously damaged. He could no longer work in the dusty surroundings of a cabinet maker's shop. But even now he had numerous tools, many pieces of wood, and a host of other instruments needed to build those wonderful things which make a child's life exciting. All those tools and supplies were carefully stored in a shed outside. Over the years, he had built many toys for me. Other kids were often jealous; they did not have a dad like mine.

My father brought two strong strips of wood from the shed. He fastened them across each other. One of the four ends was longer than the other three. He took string and tied it around the endpoints of that wooden cross. I recognized the shape: I could see that the final result of his work would indeed look like a kite! He found brown wrapping paper and glued it so it would cover both wood and string.

I helped him assemble a long tail for our kite. We tied a strong cord, maybe ten feet in length, to the longer end of our kite and knotted it around pieces of paper, placed about six inches from each other. Finally, my father fastened string to all four corners of the kite, pulled the strings together about two feet below the kite's body and tied it all together. There the long line we would hold could be attached.

I painted a face on our kite: Eyes, mouth and nose - in color, of course. The kite was ready! I could hardly wait to take it outside, but my father wanted to get a few other things first. "We need them," he mentioned casually. I could not understand the delay. I was not exactly happy that we would have to wait. But my father insisted. He put a pencil in his pocket. He found thin cardboard and cut it into small circles, about four inches in diameter, and punched a hole into the center of each circle. Finally he took scissors and very carefully made one cut from the outside of each circle to its center.

"Why do we need all that?" I was impatient. What was he doing? It seemed so irrelevant to flying a kite. I just wanted to leave.

"You'll see later." He smiled, a very secretive smile. Finally, he was done. I found a very long line which I had kept among the toys in my bedroom. It was still in its original wrapper: the printed inscription read 250 Meters. That should be enough. Two-hundred fifty meters... our kite would fly very high!

While we had been building the kite, my mother had started preparations for lunch. It was the weekend; our big meal would be eaten around noon. She was boiling white beans. They would turn into bean soup, once she added the other ingredients.

I was looking forward to that soup. It had always been one of my favorites. We grew the beans in our own garden. Carrots would be added, and potatoes, and celery. I asked my mother to go easy on the celery please, I didn't like it very much). And a few other things. There would be no meat in the soup today, none had been available from the butcher. It was war, after all. But my mother had been able to get a large marrow bone. The beans were swirling around it. Yes, I was looking forward to the soup. But I was even more looking forward to sending our kite high into the sky!

"The soup will be done in two to three hours," my mother reminded us. My father smiled and kissed her. I would have kissed her too, but I could not wait. The kite had to fly!

My father took my hand as we walked toward an open meadow, not far from the forest. We had lots of room to maneuver on this meadow. Even if the kite bounced up and down or fell to the ground, it could not get caught in wires or branches.

"A bit too much wind," my dad thought aloud. But the extra wind would not bother me! I was sure I would be strong enough to hold the line, no matter how much the kite might pull away from me!

Then, finally, the time had come. I grasped the line about ten yards from the kite and ran into the wind. The kite shot up into the air, bounced up and down, and crashed. I tried it again. And again. Finally it worked: The kite climbed a bit, tried to dive once to the left and once to the right, caught itself about five feet above the ground, its tail drawing a line through the grass, and then pulled upwards. I gave it more line. It climbed. As it moved higher above the ground, its movements became calmer, as though it was happy finally to be where it belonged. Its face stared down at us. It seemed to be saying: "You poor earthbound humans! If you only knew how great it is to fly! To be a kite! What a view!"

After I let out about two hundred meters of line, my father suggested: "Why don't we tell the kite to climb even higher?"

"It can't hear us!" I countered. "I forgot to draw ears

on the kite. So it can't hear anything."

"But you gave it eyes. I am sure the kite will be able to read!"

"Maybe, but there is nothing for it to read."

"That can be changed." He took one of those circles he had cut earlier, found the pencil in one of his pockets, and, in large letters, wrote "Please fly much higher" onto the circle. Then he guided the cut in that cardboard circle over the line that reached up to our kite, until the punched out center was caressing the line. The wind caught the cardboard and quickly pushed the circle upward. As our message reached the top, the kite, possibly hit by a sudden shift in the wind pattern, shot back and forth.

"The kite agrees!" my father reminded me, "but it cannot climb higher unless you give it more line!" I was happy to cooperate.

We sent several more letters. Either the kite enjoyed getting mail or the wind up there was increasing and shifting - the kite's flight was becoming more and more restless. The tension on the string increased. After a while, my father helped me hold the line; I could no longer do it by myself. Then, suddenly, the wind howled. The storm my father had predicted was upon us. Somewhere, between us and our kite, the line tore. I stared upwards at my beautiful kite. Where would it come down?

But it did not fall to earth. The wind was building. The kite was bouncing around, out of control, moving closer toward the forest. It continued to stay up high - maybe it was even drifting higher. It looked smaller and smaller. I could no longer recognize its face, even when the side I painted with eyes, nose and mouth would momentarily point in our direction. Maybe the kite would even fly to the next town - some three miles away. Or even further....

"Well," my father tried to comfort me, "a kite should be in the sky. I am sure it would have been unhappy if we had taken it home and put it somewhere in the corner. Now that it knows what it is like to fly, it does not want to come back to earth!"

When he saw that I was not quite persuaded, he added,

"And next time, we can always build another kite!"

I was satisfied. Besides, it was about time for lunch. I was looking forward to that wonderful white bean soup. From some storms, there are safe, secure havens.

BOMB DAMAGE

The Gerbers were staying in our guest bedroom. Their house, not far from the downtown center of Kiel, had been destroyed in yesterday's air attack. They had asked whether they could live with us for a few days. Afterwards, they would leave. But they did not yet know where they would go. It would be somewhere away from the city.

The Gerbers were old friends. Of course my parents invited them to stay with us. For that matter, they could stay as long as they would like. And I was happy that we had company. Mr Gerber knew how to tell funny stories. He could make me laugh. Mrs. Gerber was nice too. But I was much less enthusiastic about little Marie, their daughter. She refused to speak with me. Worse, she was always afraid. I liked girls. I had played with other girls who were Marie's age. But this one... somehow she reminded me of the first few words in a children's book that my parents had brought home: "Poor little Mary, little child, sensitive to every wind..."

Maybe her problems had something to do with the bombs that fell on us and on them nearly every night and day. After all, I had my own fears and nightmares. Often I could not sleep at night. When I closed my eyes, the fury of the bombs and the yellow-red fires of burning houses appeared in front of me. But at least I was not afraid of talking to people!

I asked my parents what I should do about Marie. "Just be nice to her," my mother suggested, "even if she does not speak to you. You know, their house was destroyed last night. It is completely gone, just a pile of rubble. All her toys are under the rubble. If that happened here, it would upset you too, wouldn't it?"

It would. I understood. A few days ago, I had been downtown with my parents. It was impossible to walk through many of the familiar streets. They were blocked by too much rubble from collapsed buildings. The streetcars that I loved so much would only traverse short distances: in many places, their tracks were covered with cement and bricks. You had to climb over those mounds of rubble and walk maybe half a mile to find the next streetcar. Of course, streetcars were only running when electricity was available, and that was rare.

I hated to walk past all those destroyed buildings. It was scary. Empty walls were pointing into the sky, threatening to fall as we were trying to pass by. When would our house look like that? Just the thought of it made me shudder.

Now I understood why so many people from downtown were dejectedly dragging themselves past our house, walking away from the city. Some would pull a kid's wagon, others were pushing a wheelbarrow, loaded with whatever they had saved. Yet others just walked away with nothing. They did not want to spend another night downtown. Even if they had wanted to stay, many probably had no place to sleep, except in the rubble, exposed to the hail of the bombs. Surely these people did not yet want to die.

Occasionally, some family would knock on our door exhausted, asking to stay overnight, only until tomorrow morning, when their trek away from the city - to who knows where - would continue. We let them stay, but we warned them: maybe the bombs would not fall on us as often as they did downtown, but we certainly were not safe from air attacks!

Today, the Gerbers were with us. As usual, I was told to go to bed right after dinner. Our visitors and my parents were talking and playing cards. At the time I did not know that the Gerbers and my parents were somehow both involved in the underground movement against the Nazis. In retrospect, I assume that they needed to talk about things that I was not to hear - for my own safety. All I knew was that they were playing cards, "Skat," a very popular bidding game in Germany. The game was always played by three persons: the individual with the best cards played against the other two. I did not know how they would manage it - there were four of them, but only three could play at any time! But that would be their problem.

Marie was already sleeping but I could not fall asleep. I was afraid of the fire that I would see again. It was always there, flickering, glowing, rising to giant proportions as soon as I closed my eyes. So I forced myself to keep my eyes wide open. As long as I did not close my eyes, I could see nice things like the lacy drapes covering the window or the shadow of a quince tree outside.

A bit of light filtered in. Maybe it was the moon. How much nicer than all those fires!

My mother believed that I did not want to fall asleep. "You probably think you might miss something interesting while you are sleeping, right?" But she was wrong. Some evenings, especially when I was tired, I would have loved to fall asleep. I was just too scared of the red and yellow flames!

And, soon the sirens would wail again anyway! It happened most nights. It was much harder to jump out of bed after just an hour of sleep. It was so much easier to stay awake! Somehow, the sirens were not quite as scary when I was awake.

Finally, I got up and went into the living room. In this case, I would indeed have missed something if I had not gotten up! Mr Gerber was just beginning to tell a joke.

"Hitler, Göring and Göbbels have all died," he started. His pronouncement generated wild enthusiasm. After all, those three were among the most infamous leaders of the Nazi movement: Hitler the "Führer" of it all, Göring, his designated successor and Göbbels, the super-propagandist, whose repeated false assertions were presented so well that many people believed whatever lies he invented.

"No, no," Mr Gerber waved his hands, "I am not finished. Anyway, the three died and got to the gates of heaven. As usual, the gatekeeper on duty was St. Peter. As you know, he is the one who decides whether someone will be allowed in or not. But before Peter could even say a word, Hitler insists: "Open the gates!"

But Peter was not impressed. "Not so fast," he answers "up here everything is done at its own pace. Besides, who are you anyway?"

"I am Adolf Hitler, the great leader of Greater Germany!"

"Oh," says Peter. "We have heard of you up here. Made lots of trouble down there, didn't you! Well, we may let you in after a while. We are great on forgiveness up here. But first, tell me how many times in life you have lied."

Hitler had to think a while about that one. "If I remember correctly, 25,731 times."

St. Peter looked astonished: "That often? That is more than once a day! Well, anyway, you will have to jog 25,731 times around the perimeter of heaven. It will take you quite a while! When you are done, I will let you in."

He turned to Göring: "What about you? What is your name and how often did you lie?"

"I am the Reichs Marshall Hermann Göring!" The fat, bejeweled man in boots and uniform slowly moved his head back and forth. "How many times have I lied? I can't count. At least 40,000 times."

Peter stared and slowly shook his head. "Forty thousand? Besides, you are no longer a Reichs Marshall. Up here you are just another soul. I'll accept the 40,000. Who knows whether you'll ever finish that one. Well, you know what to do!"

Göring started to take off after Hitler, beginning the first round to circle heaven. But Peter called him back: "Wait a minute! What happened to that third one, the little guy?"

Göring chuckled. "Him? That is Göbbels. He lied more than any of us. He is probably on the way back to earth to get his motorcycle. He'll need it!"

Mr. Gerber's last words were hardly audible. The wail of the sirens had started. My father turned on the radio and switched to the phone line station. It was ticking. So far, the alarm was only an early warning. The ticking stopped and the announcer calmly mentioned that enemy aircraft were approaching from directly west of us at the North-Sea coast. Would they attack us or turn south to Hamburg? Were they on their way to Berlin?

The sirens started to howl again. Full alarm! The planes were heading for Kiel. "Christmas trees" lit up the sky. The colored markers indicating ground zero followed. One hit the earth about three hundred feet from our house. It was once more our turn! We ran down the stairs to the basement. Food and water had been stored there. Benches were set up. If necessary, we could survive down there for a few days, just in case the house should collapse above us. But if the house would burn or if there would be a direct hit by an explosive bomb, that would be it!

I was scared. Marie was crying. The adults hardly talked. We were sitting and waiting.

We heard the bombs. Wavering howls and whistles. Then detonations. The house shook a little. It was quiet again. Was it over?

Mr. Gerber asked whether any of us had heard about the guy from Kiel who had to go to the bathroom during an air attack.

"No, we are not usually informed when someone downtown needs to use the toilet." My father was joking.

"I know, I know, but this was not quite normal. I thought maybe you might have heard. So let me tell you. Of course, I am not sure whether the story happened exactly as I was told. I don't know the man. Supposedly he lived one street over from us, you know, on that block where all the apartment buildings collapsed during an air attack three weeks ago."

"Anyway, he had diarrhea. With that horrible food we get these days, stomach problems are common. But it was during the night. The bombs were coming down and he had to go to the bathroom. And there was no bathroom in their basement. He could not wait. So he had no choice but to go upstairs, despite the bombs. He had been gone about two minutes, when some bombs hit the building. The noise was incredible. Walls must have collapsed above. Stucco fell from the basement ceiling. Everyone knew he would be dead. Killed by his diarrhea."

"When the air attack was over, the people in the basement used hands and shovels to free a passage through the rubble to get upstairs. When they finally made it outside, they heard crazy laughter. It was the man with the stomach problem. He was still sitting on the toilet on the second floor. The wall between him and the street was gone. The staircase he used to go upstairs was also gone. They could see from the street that he was still sitting on the toilet, laughing and laughing."

"'For God's sake, why are you laughing?' someone yelled upwards."

35

"'You won't believe it,' the man on the toilet responded. 'When I flushed, the wall fell down!'"

One of us laughed about Mr. Gerber's story; the rest listened to the detonations that had started once again. The explosions seemed to come ever closer. Marie was crying. "It must be a formation of Angels that is dropping bombs, one bomb after another," someone announced. We listened. That is what it was. We had started to call them "bomb carpets." The craters would cover a designated area on the ground, maybe a square mile or so, leaving little if anything standing, certainly leaving nothing undamaged.

The detonations continued to come closer and closer. Long howling, thumping detonations. The next time the howl was louder but shorter, the detonation much louder. Still shorter and louder. All of us knew - about another ten seconds, and we would be either alive or dead. Nine seconds, eight. Very loud explosions. The house shakes. Seven, six. A very short howl. A wild explosion. I am scared. Five, four. No more howling, just the incredible noise. Paint falls from the walls. Panic on all faces. Three, two. It thunders like never before. I can no longer tell the explosions apart. It is all one endless unbearable noise! I am shaking! Part of the basement ceiling drops down. Two, one, I hold my hands over my ears and hide my face in my mother's dress. Sudden darkness. Incredible noise. Everything is wildly shaking back and forth. Something is rolling down the stairs to the basement. I think I am screaming, but I am not sure.

Then it is over. We are still alive. This time, anyway.

Someone suggests that the house next door must have collapsed. Or the old barn in back. Someone else is sure that our house, right above this basement, is no longer standing. Mr. Gerber mentions that it is good that none of us had to go to the bathroom. But nobody seems to appreciate his humor. His comment does not seem funny.

My father climbed past the debris on the steps to look for incendiary bombs. When he returned he said, "The house is still standing. But there is a lot of damage."

Two hours later, the air attack ends. We climb over debris to go up the steps and look around.

All over the house, window glass was shattered. Roof tiles were lying on the ground outside. Close to the house was a new giant crater where a tree once stood. Doors were torn from their hinges. Furniture, broken and mangled, was piled in corners of several rooms. Drapes were ripped, pictures had been blown off the walls. But the house stood.

The most incredible thing, however, was a round hole in a lead crystal dish. Our living room adjoined the dining room; they were divided by a large and very heavy sliding double door that traveled on steel ball bearings. Each of these steel balls was about three-quarters of an inch in diameter. Both doors had been blown out of place. The steel balls had exploded outward like bullets, hitting various objects in the living room. One of them had passed through the crystal dish, then through the oak table below. Strangely enough, neither the dish nor the table had moved much out of place. Even more strangely, the bowl had not shattered. The force must have been incredible: the bowl had a perfectly circular hole, as though someone had carefully drilled it.

Maybe it was good, after all, that nobody had gone to the bathroom when those bombs had hit.

TEARS

I was not popular with some of my classmates, especially some who were considerably older. Several among them had repeated grades more than once. Three students - my best friend Friedrich-Karl, a pretty girl with the name Anne-Lene, and I usually knew the answers to the teacher's questions. A few other students did not do badly; they got by. Those who were not so quick were repeatedly beaten by the teacher simply because they did not do as well as we did. Just before hitting them with his bamboo stick, the teacher would point out that they should follow our example. Not surprisingly, they tried to get back at us whenever they could.

Sometimes their aggression was pretty harmless. I remember, for example, that one girl took the cap my mother made me wear. She ran away with it. I presume she took it all the way to her home in a small town about two miles away. I followed her for a couple of blocks and quickly gave up. She was older and faster than I. I did not like that cap anyway! Surely it would take my parents a while to get a new cap for me. After all, clothing was scarce. I was in luck. I went to school without having to wear that dreadful cap for quite a few weeks!

However, the older boys were sometimes especially nasty. One day, they brought a broomstick to school. When school was over for the day, one of them approached me from behind. I did not see him. He quickly stuck the stick between my legs. Another kid picked it up in front of me and they both lifted up. Once the broomstick touched my groin, they started bouncing it up and down. It hurt! I started to cry.

After a while they stopped their nasty game. They had achieved their goal. I limped home, tears in my eyes. A man in full Nazi uniform saw me and crossed the street to confront me. "Are you crying?" he shouted. And then, in a tone of complete disgust he added, "German boys don't cry. You are acting like a little girl. You will be a bad German if you don't stop!" He walked off.

When I arrived home, I told my mother what had happened. She gently shook her head when she heard the Nazi's

words. "There is a poem," she told me, "with a few lines that
you may want to remember as long as you live:
'Cry,
Never will a tear dishonor the most noble face.
To cry is honorable, yet
To succumb to sadness is not.'"

A VISITOR FROM STRALSUND

My grandmother, my mother's mother, arrived from Stralsund to visit us. She was a noble woman who had grown up in a wealthy family. Born in 1873, she married an important royal official whose father and grandfather had been captains of clipper ships. In short, she considered herself important.

I had trouble getting along with her. In the fairy tales I had read, grandmothers either were witches or gentle, loving, and caring old ladies. Mine was not gentle. And, it seemed to me, not at all loving. Maybe it was all due to the period when she had grown up: Women at the time were beginning to look for independence. Yet they were supposed to be completely dependent on the whims of their husbands. My grandmother had faced such problems. On the other hand, maybe the problem was just a warped personality, that of a spoiled child who never quite grew up.

I am sure that it was difficult for anyone to live with her. She was divorced from my grandfather. Even though they continued to love each other, they could not live together. My mother had told me about my grandparents' divorce. The two of them had walked into the divorce court holding hands. Their attorney had to stop them: "The judge will never give you a divorce if you keep holding hands!" he had insisted. They complied and the judge let them go their separate ways.

My mother did not have a pleasant childhood. Later on, my grandmother had strongly objected to my parents' marriage. "You are from a good family!" she had argued with my mother. "You cannot marry a Senator! My God, he is a politician! You have to marry someone of your own status!"

My father had been elected to the German national legislature, the Reichstag, during the 1920s. It was the time of the ill-fated Weimar Republic, before the Nazis took power. The Reichstag had only one chamber; it was somewhat more "Senate" than "House of Representatives."

Worse than being a senator, as far as my grandmother was concerned, my father was a Social Democrat. Such a party would not fight for the wealthy or for the welfare of the nobility.

But even if he had been a strict conservative, in her eyes - and in the view of so many of her kind - he would have been an outcast. Among the upper class, many felt that dealing in politics was degrading. Politics, to her and to many other Germans, was considered dirty - good people should not be involved in government.

The government should have been left to the emperor. Unfortunately, Kaiser Wilhelm had left Germany at the end of the First World War. She believed that if the royalty had stayed, there would have been no "dirty Nazis."

Somehow, once my parents had married against her will, and once she got to know him well, my grandmother changed her mind about my father. But, her overall personality never changed. To me, she continued to be more of a witch than anything else.

As a child, I rarely saw her. I felt quite fortunate that she lived far away. My mother was very different from my grandmother - always loving, leaving me enough freedom to explore my world, as long as I was not trying to do something dangerous. My grandmother's views about children, however, were diametrically opposed to those of my mother. On those few occasions when we visited her in the old Hanseatic city of Stralsund, or like this time, when she was visiting us, she behaved as though she was both emperor and dictator.

She stood straight, still very attractive despite her age. Her face was set, her eyes hard. Even though her waist had increased from 26 to something like 36 inches over the years, she still looked like authority personified.

"Why are you playing with your trains?" she demanded to know. Then, without even waiting for my answer, she added with force in her voice: "Put the trains away. Play with your blocks!" An hour later, she would demand that I put the blocks away and take out my trains. Again, something like an hour later, her orders changed again. She would never let me finish anything. She was driving me crazy! I wished she would leave!

But then I discovered how I could upset her. As demanded, I disassembled the trains and carefully put them away. She would have tolerated nothing less. Then I took out the blocks. First, I built a very tall, very beautiful building. Then I took several blocks and placed them lengthwise end-to-end. Toward the middle, I constructed another end-to-end set of blocks to make a large cross. Next, I went to ask my mother for a long and strong rubber band. She used rubber band rings from time to time to conserve vegetables from our garden. They were placed between the cover and the body of giant glass jars to seal those jars. There were always a few rubber band rings that she would no longer use; those that had gotten old and would no longer seal the jars reliably.

I took one of those rings and carefully stretched it around the four corners of the cross I had constructed, just like my father had done with string when he built my kite. It was not easy; the blocks always wanted to slide out of place. But with a bit of patience it could be done. Finally it worked. My bomb was ready.

After all, it was war. I knew exactly how bombs fall diagonally into buildings below. So I threw the cross-bomb toward the ground, hitting the parquet floor exactly at the base of my beautiful tall building. The bomb blew apart. Its blocks, accelerated by the contracting rubber band, flew in several directions. Many hit my building. It collapsed with the appropriate noise. I laughed loudly.

My grandmother was furious. "You can't do that!" she yelled, red with anger.

"Why not? It is not a real house - it is just blocks!"

She did not know how to answer. How could a child even dare to ask why something would not be allowed? Wasn't it enough when an adult simply states that some behavior is not acceptable? Why was an explanation needed? Children are supposed to obey, nothing else!

She immediately asserted her authority. "Put those blocks back. Play with your trains. I want you to play with your trains all day. I don't want to see those blocks again!"

I took out the trains. This time I could finish my train setup. That was, after all, what I had wanted to achieve all along.

THE LATE WAR YEARS

CRAZY

Somewhere to the northeast of us, out in the beautiful countryside that has been called the "Switzerland of Holstein," nestled between hills and forests and lakes, was a very large farm. It was no more than 10 miles from where we lived, but far enough from the city to be out of danger. The owner of that farm was always extremely well dressed, even though by 1942 clothing was no longer available in those few stores that had not yet been destroyed. We could not figure out how he was able to live so well. Maybe, it had something to do with the "crazy one," the wealthy farmer's employee and helper in many things.

We only saw the "crazy one" when he came into our suburb. He always sat on the seat of a wooden wagon, drawn by two beautiful horses. Sometimes he would bring large containers filled with milk to the local dairy. There must have been many cows on that farm! At other times he came to buy groceries. The farmer's family, if there was one, never came. They always sent the "crazy one."

Someone insisted that the farmer was actually a psychiatrist. The "crazy one," supposedly rode the wagon into town for therapy. But nobody could say whether that story was true.

We always knew a few minutes in advance when the "crazy one" would pass by our house. He made sure everybody knew. He cracked his whip above the horses, but he never hit them. He screamed words that nobody could understand. He seemed to enjoy his own screaming. Somehow, he found it amusing that everybody watched him. For the local people it was a good thing. It gave them something to talk about, something that had nothing to do with the war and with the houses that had been bombed out last night. And whatever you said about the "crazy one," such remarks could not be interpreted as statements against the government. In other words, it was safe to talk about him. Several people in town were sure that the Nazi government consisted of people that were just as crazy, but you could not talk about that. Whenever anyone did, the Nazis would arrest that person and chop off his head.

In the center of our town, there were four small grocery

stores and a butcher shop. All the stores were quite small; maybe eight to ten customers would fit inside. The sales ladies worked behind a counter. They would go into the back room to get whatever a customer wanted. Of course, they could only get it whenever there was a supply. At this time in the war, most things were no longer available.

My mother had sent me grocery shopping. She had given me the money and the needed food ration stamps. I had taken a small bag with me; the little food we would get for our ration stamps would easily fit into that bag. I was prepared to go from one store to another until I had found something that we could eat that day. I had entered the first store and was waiting my turn. Some lady customer in front of me asked for cheese - any kind of cheese. There was no cheese. But she was told about a rumor that there may be some cheese next week. "I believe it is supposed to be Tilsiter cheese," the sales woman guessed. "But you can't rely on that. With all those air attacks, you never know what will get here and what will be destroyed on the way here."

The customer's next question got a different answer. "No, we don't have any flour, but you can get farina for the same food stamps. Up to half a pound. Is that what you want?" Yes, she wanted the farina. Gladly. She had intended to ask for some other items as well, but she did not get the chance to ask. Just then, the "crazy one" pushed himself into the store. He shoved people aside to get to the counter. I would have been next in line, but I did not mind waiting. I wanted to see what would happen.

He did not say much. He screamed a few incomprehensible syllables. Then he threw a piece of paper onto the counter. The paper was followed by food stamps, by special stamps only for those who went on authorized trips. "There!" he yelled. And then he pounded with his hand on the piece of paper. "That!"

The owner of the store felt obviously uncomfortable. Her face had turned rather white. She treated the "crazy one" very, very carefully. "We don't have any flour, any kind of flour," she said gently, "and you don't have any ration stamps for flour either."

"That!" the "crazy one" yelled. He punched the piece of paper with his finger. Then he pointed the same finger at the lady who owned the store. "You! That!"

He had clearly made his point. He turned his head and studied the other customers. Most of them looked shy and a little afraid. Nobody would bother him. But I found his behavior much more interesting than frightening. I smiled a little. He seemed to notice that I did not react like the others. At first, he looked surprised and a bit uncertain. Surely he recognized that I was only a child. For an instant, there seemed to be a bit of light in his eyes. Did he smile at me in a strange way? Now he turned back to the counter and yelled even louder: "That!!!"

The lady on the other side of the counter appeared even paler than before. "But we don't have any flour," she whispered. Her voice sounded as though she was begging. He would not stop. He began to scream those incomprehensible syllables. Finally, the lady went to the room in back and brought him a bag of flour. The "crazy one" got everything else on his list. He pushed the ration stamps and the money off the counter. It fell onto the floor, at the feet of the lady who had given him the groceries he demanded. Then he turned, walked out of the door and cracked his whip a few times as he climbed onto his wagon. He snapped the reins of his horses up and down, whistled, seemed to sing briefly, then yelled and left. We could hear his screams fade into the distance.

The lady who had been offered farina instead of flour was angry. "So you did have flour!" she glared. "I want flour, not farina!"

"No, I don't have flour," answered the store's owner. "That was my own. I had saved it for two weeks! Now I can't bake a cake. Tomorrow is my son's birthday and I had saved the flour to bake a cake for him. Now it is useless. But what could I do, I had to get rid of that crazy idiot!"

Now I understood why the farmer sent the "crazy one" to go shopping. And I wondered about something else: How crazy is that "crazy one?" An idiot he certainly was not.

THE AIR-RAID GOOSE

All of us tried to make up for the scarcity of food by growing our own produce. Gardens became very popular. Flowers were replaced with vegetables. Female sheep and goats were raised to get a little milk. The sound of chickens could be heard behind most houses in the suburbs. We had a large garden. We had chickens, and we raised rabbits. The extra food helped us to live through long periods of overall deprivation.

My best friend's family did things just a bit differently. They owned a garden with many fruit and nut trees. Below the trees grazed a sheep. And all around the sheep fluttered a flock of geese.

All but one of those geese had been bought as little chicks on the very same day. One single chick arrived about a week later. It became the outcast. The other geese would have nothing to do with the newcomer. This one, even after it grew up, had to spend its time by itself, usually far away from the others and from my friend's house, way on the other end of their garden.

But there was something unusual about this goose - she understood the meaning of air raid sirens. Whenever the sirens wailed, the flock of geese would not be disturbed. The single outcast, however, would immediately stretch its neck and would race toward the house with wildly flapping wings. It would make its way through the open basement door and relax only after the entire family was assembled, after it had joined its humans in the safest room of the basement. There it would wait with everyone until the raid was over. The other geese, in contrast, remained exposed to the bombs.

But, alas, even the wise goose did not survive. Like the others, one day, it was served as Sunday dinner.

ARCH OF FIRE

Yesterday's attack on Kiel had lasted for several hours. All night long, the sky to our west had been a bright yellow-red. The city was burning. Sometimes it looked as though the glow in the sky flickered just a little. Maybe some bomb was exploding a bit late. Judging from the direction of the brightness, we concluded that downtown Kiel must be on fire.

My father was quite concerned about his office. All his important papers were there. In the morning, the three of us took the train into town. It was a weekend and I did not have to be in school - I was happy to go along. I wanted to see what had happened. I loved some of the buildings in the old downtown part of the city, especially a beautiful church and the old city hall, both built hundreds of years ago.

The city of Kiel had joined the Hanseatic League, a powerful group of trading cities, about the year 1250. Its most ancient structures were built in the style common to Hanseatic cities in the north of Europe. Although Kiel in those earlier times never achieved the stature of such places as Hamburg or Lübeck, buildings from that period still told of the past grandeur of the Hanseatic League, of cities that escaped much of the unpleasantness of life during the dark ages.

My love was not reserved entirely for the oldest structures. Newer buildings, for example, the university that had been founded in 1667 were just as attractive, even though in a quite different way. Of course, I did not know the "names" of architectural styles at that time. All I knew was that I liked the way these buildings looked. Could any of them have been damaged yesterday? I fervently hoped not! So far, they had withstood the hail of the bombs. I wanted to make sure.

We arrived at the main train station around ten in the morning, climbing over rubble to walk towards downtown. A few buildings were still smoking from last night's fires, but not many had been hit. My father pointed to a few apartment houses that had been destroyed by explosive bombs. They had still been in relatively good shape the day before. I would not have known which of the rubble heaps were new, except that the new ones spilled far into the street. There had not yet been time to clear enough of the streets to let traffic get by. But, overall, it looked as though the major damage from yesterday's attack had not been downtown. Someone told us that most of the destruction was just a bit to the south of city center. Blocks and blocks of apartments in that area had been completely wiped out.

As we approached the old church at the very center of the downtown district, air raid sirens began to wail. It was a different sound than the one I knew. Our suburban town had only one siren. It was loud enough for all of us to hear. But in Kiel there were many, all howling at the same time. Some were closer, others more or less distant from where we were walking at the moment. Their howls did not reach us quite at the same time. The ups and downs of the wails were cacophonous, making the threat they promised even more eerie.

We quickly walked to the nearest bunker. My father knew its location; it was only three blocks from his office. He had spent hours in that place on many occasions, every time a daytime air attack had forced him to leave his office. The bunker we were approaching looked like a huge, grey, concrete block, four stories above and four more stories below ground. Its walls were enormously thick. No bomb, no matter how large, would ever be able to break through those walls.

As we arrived at the entrance, we could already hear the sound of the planes. I was frightened. I was much more frightened than I would have been at home! Somehow this was different. I did not know why or how it was different. It was unfamiliar. It was so strange!

The brown shirted man at the entrance directed us to the top floor. I refused to go. I wanted to go down, just like at home, where we would go down into our basement. The deeper underground, the better.

"It is already full down there!" the uniformed man said. My father persuaded him to let us go downstairs nonetheless. "Don't worry, we will find a place." We did.

People were sitting on benches. The air was damp and fetid. Someone was sick. Grown-ups just sat there. The silence was broken only by the pitiful cries of a frightened little girl.

49

Most of the adults did not speak. They stared into space. Even men in Nazi uniforms just stared. The few people who occasionally did say something would only whisper to each other.

Suddenly the benches began to shake. I heard a vague thumping noise. A few people screamed. The bombs were falling around us! In this part of downtown! The bunker was hit several times. Again and again it shook. But it held. I started crying too. This was too strange, too new, too threatening. I understood that I was safer in this bunker than I would ever be in the basement at home, but it made no difference! I wanted to be home!

After about three hours, it was over. We were allowed to leave the bunker. My parents and I climbed the steps with all the other people. Now everyone was talking. Everyone was afraid of what they might see outside. People feared for their apartments, for their stores, for the little possessions they had left. Had this air attack finally destroyed it all?

As we emerged, we felt the heat of fires around us. Flames were everywhere. My father wanted to get to his office as quickly as he could. Again we climbed over rubble towards the old church. We would have to pass by the church, cross the old market, walk past the old city hall and then turn right. My father's office would be a few houses down the next street. But when we came close to the church, I would not go further.

A relatively narrow street separated the church from a five-story department store across the street. Both the church and the store were on fire. Flames shot out of the windows into the street. It was hot! And above the street was an arch of fire! Flames from the church and flames from the department store joined above the street to shoot hundreds of feet into the sky.

"We must get through there!" my father urged. Some other people dared to run underneath the fiery arch. I did not want to go. It was too scary. I just wanted to go home! I began to cry again. It was so awful! I could not stand it!

After another minute my parents somehow got me to run through the fire arch with them. Underneath that arch it was incredibly hot. Air streamed in from behind us, rising toward the flames above us as we ran through the arch of fire. Suddenly I could not feel the street under my feet. The rushing air was lifting me upwards toward the flames. It was the beginning of a fire storm. My parents, heavier than I, were holding my hands, one on each side, holding me down. We got through! I was shaking, chilled with intense fear, despite the heat. I absolutely would go no further.

Beyond the arch of fire we now stood in the old market place. I turned to look back. My church was on fire! My old city hall had turned to rubble! I could not move. No amount of persuasion would make me take another step toward those fires. My parents tried. Finally, my father went ahead by himself. He raced the next couple of hundred feet toward his office. His building was burning! He needed to save his files! Frustrated with me he thought, "If I could only have been here a minute or two earlier, I could be half done collecting the important files!"

Finally he reached the building and opened the outside door. The fire had already reached the entry to the building. As he was about to run inside, the ceiling crashed down into the hallway.

All he could do is walk back to us. He had arrived too late. As I saw him, he was smiling at me. "Thank you for slowing me down!" he said. I did not know what he meant until he explained later that evening.

The entire downtown area was on fire. Most streets were not passable. We had to criss-cross back and forth to find a way to the train station. But there were no trains: the railroad station was also burning. Debris was lying all over the tracks. There would be no more trains today. We had to walk home.

It was a strange walk. I was a child and could not walk fast. It took more than four hours to get home. Most of the way we were reminded of where we had just been. Soot and small blackened bits of paper kept drifting down on us. Those grim reminders continued to rain from the sky long after we had left the flames behind.

THE PERILS OF A HANDICAP

March 1943. We received a special delivery letter from an aunt in Pomerania. She was desperate. Her son Willi had applied for a marriage license. As was the rule for all couples, to obtain permission to wed, he and his fiancee had to appear in person at the state "health offices." After interviewing Willi and his girlfriend the Nazi official denied their license and inquired where the two of them could be found during the next few days. Shortly thereafter my aunt received an official letter indicating that her son would be "relocated."

Both Willi and the woman he loved were mentally handicapped. As a child, Willi had fallen down a steep flight of stairs and crashed his head into a stone wall. He had been in a coma for several days: brain damage. Nonetheless, he had grown up to be a responsible and nice young man, albeit a bit limited in mental capacity. His intended wife had experienced her own trauma. As a teenager she had been in an automobile accident. Her mental capacity had suffered as well. The two of them functioned at about the same level. They understood and loved each other. They had decided to marry. But the government would have none of it.

The Nazis publicly announced that anyone with a genetic flaw would not be allowed to have children. Such people could not marry. But the Nazis had not told the public that they had instituted a much more severe policy. Handicapped persons would be relocated to concentration camps. The Nazis government wanted to assure that "Aryan racial purity" would be assured by the proliferation of perfect genes. While we did not know then that Willi's relocation would mean death, my aunt but especially my parents still feared for his fate.

My parents composed a letter that my aunt's family sent to their health department. It emphasized that Willi's problem had been generated by an injury during childhood. The letter explained that all other members of our family were mentally and physically healthy and generally lived to a very old age. If genetic problems existed, other individuals should have been affected as well.

52

Somehow the letter had the intended effect. The health department requested certification from the physicians who had treated Willi and the woman he intended to marry. Both doctors assured the government that the handicap had been entirely due to injury.

Permission to marry was granted. However - on order of the health department both Willi and his future wife were forcibly sterilized prior to their wedding date to assure that they could not produce "inferior" offspring.

THE DEBATING GAME

"The Nazis don't make sense," I announced over dinner. "The teacher told us that the English are stupid because they did not join Germany to fight some of the other countries. It doesn't make sense!"

My mother seemed amused by my sudden outburst. "But that kind of thinking does make sense to the Nazis!"

"How can it? Why should they join the Nazi war? They have no reason to!"

At home, we often talked about our reasons for hating the Nazi point of view. On the other hand, I was forced to listen to Nazi propaganda in school. The differING viewpoints were unreconcilable. I had started to reject anything the teacher said about that topic without even thinking about it.

"I think it would be better if you understood why they are thinking and acting the way they are." My father looked gently at me. "Their way of thinking is not very complicated. You are still a child, but a child can understand how they think. Let us play a little game. We will have a debate. You, Siegfried, will argue the Nazi point of view. Mommy and I will argue against it. All right?"

"I don't want to argue for the Nazis! Everything they do is bad! I don't think that way! I don't want to talk that way either!"

"Just try it. It is just a game!"

"But it is an awful game!"

"Not really. It is called a debate. People used to do that kind of thing all the time until the Nazis forbade it. Just try it, please!"

I finally agreed, even though I felt uncomfortable. I hated to say things that I could not believe in. I hated even more to argue for things that hurt people!

"Fine. Now, Siegfried, what was it that the teacher said?"

"He said that England should fight on the side of Germany. I guess against Russia. Maybe even against France. I don't know."

"Why would the Nazis think that England should be on their side?"

"Well, the English are Germanic people. They are like us. Most of them came from Angeln in Schleswig-Holstein and from Lower Saxony on the North Coast of Germany."

"I don't see why that makes them so special. Why is it important that they are Germanic people? The Danes are too, so are the Swedes and the Norwegians. Why is it important?"

"That is what is so stupid about it."

My mother interceded. "You are supposed to argue their point of view, not just call it stupid. Why is it so stupid?"

I thought about it for a while. "Supposedly Germanic people are special. They are more...... They are Aryans."

"What does that mean?"

"I guess they come from a different race."

"Fine. Hitler does not look like an Aryan. Neither does Göbbels and several others among the Nazi leaders. But let us not worry about that. What is so special about the Aryan race?"

I had a difficult time coming up with an answer. The Nazis just said these people were special. Supposedly they were more worthy than other people. Supposedly they were born to rule the world. "I guess, if all Aryans are better and more intelligent than other people, then it would be better for them to make all the important decisions in the world."

"I am not sure that is reasonable. But even if it were, how do you know they are better? Look, a lot of important inventions, beautiful music, great books have come from countries that are not Aryan. Italy, France, Russia, Japan, China, and so on. And several great Germans were not Aryans either: they were Jews! So why are the Aryans more intelligent?"

"My teacher said that they are."

"And how does your teacher know that?"

"He did not tell us how he knows. He probably just believes it. Maybe it makes him feel good because he looks like an Aryan."

"And maybe he believes it because the Nazis have said it over and over and over again."

Something began to get clearer to me. Maybe this

teacher just believed it because he had been told it over and over again, until - to him - it became a truth, never to be questioned. And that one thing changed everything else. It influenced all his other thoughts and beliefs. If I would ask him why England should join Germany in the war against Russia, he would say that the English are Aryans and the Russians are not. To him that would be completely logical. But somewhere underneath all that was an idea, a belief he had never examined.

My father nudged me. "So, are the Aryans better than other people?" I thought of the Russian prisoners of war that were working for the farmer next door. They were nice people. Some among them seemed to be quite intelligent. Some of them were fun to talk with.

"I don't see any reason why we are better than other people!"

"Exactly," my mother smiled warmly. "Then should the English fight on the side of the Nazis?"

"No!"

"But why not?"

"Because Hitler and his party want to destroy other countries and rule people that don't want to be ruled by him. And because they want to get rid of people that are not Aryans. Because the Nazis are wrong when they think that other people are no good."

"One more question. If it were true that Aryans are the only good and intelligent people in the world, if all other people were not much better than monkeys, would the things the Nazis do be right? Would it make sense?"

"No, it would still not be good. You don't kill monkeys. But what they say would make a bit more sense if it were true."

"See, Siegfried, that is the problem. They believe something that is wrong and they build their points of view on it. To them it all makes sense. They even think it justifies the horrible things they do. That is why they are so dangerous! When people say things that do not make sense to you, ask them why they are believing what they believe. After a while you will get to the basis of their beliefs. Then you can decide whether their views make sense - no matter whether those points of view make sense to them."

It was a revelation. Now I could see why they were arguing the way they did. It all depended on some belief somewhere. Something that they just accepted as true, something they would never question. My father added, "It is not just the Nazis who do that kind of thing. Other people do, too. They just think something is true and everything else follows from that. To find out why they believe what they do, you have to ask them. And, remember, if they don't tell you right away, ask them over and over again. After a while you get to the basis of what they believe."

I learned a lot from that one debate. I learned not to simply reject the beliefs of other people but rather to seek where those beliefs came from. I no longer simply rejected others' views as "wrong" whenever they disagreed with my own. I learned to be more tolerant. And, with a bit of practice, I found that even a child could discover the basis of most people's attitudes. Most people's thinking, it turned out, was not very complicated. Best of all, however, I learned that understanding why the Nazis thought the way they did allowed me to beat them at their own game whenever they tried to question me about the views of my parents. I could understand their thoughts and motives without revealing my own beliefs or those of my parents.

GERMANY

Somewhere in Germany, the Nazis were celebrating their victories. The broadcast was on every radio station. The yells of "Sieg-Heil," the hostile, loud speeches, the martial music. I was wondering how real it all was. When they held such a "celebration" in Kiel, they removed many people from the local population away from the main street. Local people were mostly replaced with loyal Nazis along the route Hitler would take. It was safer for Hitler. The population of Kiel could not be trusted. But then, it was probably the same in many other cities. I had been told that, shortly before Hitler's take-over of power, he had wanted to stay in a hotel in Bonn. Not a single hotel would accept him. He had to travel miles away to Cologne to get a room. So how real was the celebration that they were broadcasting? It was hard to know.

I was at a friend's house. We were playing with trains. The volume of their radio in the living room had been turned up; his mother wanted to listen from the kitchen. All of it sounded very unpleasant to me. Finally, it ended when they played the national anthem "Deutschland, Deutschland über alles..." followed by the Nazi anthem called the 'Horst Wessel Lied.' "Die Fahne hoch..."

Over dinner at home, I told my parents that I did not like what I had heard. My parents understood; they refused to listen to Nazi celebrations. But when I included the German anthem in my negative feelings, they objected.

"See, Siegfried," my father explained, "the Nazis have tried to change the meaning of the anthem. They argue that the words 'Germany above everything' means that Germany should rule the world. That is not what the text means. It says that we love this country more than anything. Not the government we have now. Just the country and its people. Most Germans are basically good people. But they don't understand what is going on. They cannot find out what is really going on. They are not allowed to listen to anything but Nazi radio or read anything but Nazi papers. All they get is Nazi propaganda."

And my mother added, "Let us get back to the national

anthem. I don't want you to misunderstand it. The music for
the anthem was written by Josef Haydn. It is taken from one of
his string quartets. And the text is by Hoffmann von Fallersleben,
a poet. Neither of them wanted to conquer the world! Fallersleben just wanted to see Germany united. Only a hundred years
ago, Germany consisted of more than a hundred different
countries, all with their own governments. The poet loved his
country, that is why he wrote the text. 'Germany over everything' meant that we should have one country, a single country
for all the Germans, rather than lots of little principalities.
Maybe," she added, "the third verse of the German national
anthem will give you a better idea of what the poet meant. It is
a verse that the Nazis like to ignore:

'Unity, Justice and Freedom
For the German Fatherland
Let us all strive for it,
Like brothers, hand in hand.
Unity, Justice and Freedom
Are the foundation of happiness
Flourish in the aura of that happiness,
Flourish, German fatherland.'"

I liked those words. They did not advocate conquering
the world or waging war. Justice and freedom were things the
Nazis did not allow. But I also wanted to know about that other
song they always added: "Die Fahne hoch" (Raise the flag high).
"That is a fighting song," my father spoke again. "They
did not invent it; they copied it from other movements that were
fighting the Nazis. They just changed a couple of words. But
that one they ruined by making it the Nazi anthem. I don't think
I ever want to hear it again. But the German national anthem, I
hope and wish that one day its true meaning will again be
understood."[1]

---

[1] Today's democratic Germany uses the same anthem with the
quoted third verse as the official text.

ALICE

This time, it had been American planes. At night, it was usually the British. The next day, it would be the Americans. Fortunately, this attack did not last long. Maybe they had to save some of the bombs for another city.

Nonetheless, several houses were on fire. The blazes were visible from blocks away. We smelled the moist smoke that rises when people's dreams, when all they have saved for many years, when all their hard work goes up in flames. The farm of the Möllemann family was on fire. The barn could not be saved: the stored hay had turned into an inferno. One of the incendiary bombs must have ended up in the hay, another had lodged in the straw thatched roof. Straw roofs burned like a box of matches!

But the Möllemann's home was also burning. It had a straw roof as well, but that was not where the bomb had hit. Apparently a phosphorous canister had crashed diagonally through a kitchen window. That is where the flames had started. The fire department came too late. It had been busy somewhere else. Neighbors were carrying furniture and clothing out of the house. The firemen were trying to save at least part of the building. If that would not be possible, they would at least slow the progress of the flames while people saved whatever furnishings they could carry.

But then the fire reached the straw thatched roof. The flames suddenly darted up to the sky. The fireman in charge would not let anyone back inside. "Too hot and too dangerous!" he yelled.

At this point, the Möllemann family and their neighbors could only stand outside and watch. Martha Möllemann looked around for her children. Klaus and Gert stood next to their father. "Alice!" she called. No answer. Again: "Alice!!!"

Nothing. The neighbors looked around, disturbed, shocked. All three kids had just been out here! Where is that little girl? Where did she go?

She was nowhere to be seen. Suddenly, Mrs. Möllemann screamed and ran towards the front door of their burning home. But a fireman grabbed her and would not let her go. She

screamed louder. Her husband touched her. "No Martha, no."
Tears stood in his eyes. "No, Martha, I don't want to lose you!"
But she did not hear him. "Alice! Alice! Alice!"
Still nothing.

Then, at the door of the burning house, the small face of
a child appeared. Her hair seemed a little singed. "Mommy...."
She was holding a small kitten in her arms as she ran toward her
mother. Mrs. Möllemann drew the child close to her, just as the
burning roof crashed into the house.

INTERROGATION

Once again it was winter. In the morning, the sun would not rise until about nine o'clock. My father usually went to work while it was still dark. His train for downtown left at seven fourteen. This morning, he had not yet eaten breakfast when the doorbell rang. My mother opened the door; it was the local policeman.

"I am supposed to take you downtown," he said to my father. "But go ahead and finish your breakfast. We can take the seven something o'clock train. We'll still get there on time."

My mother was obviously upset. Her hands trembled as she put breakfast on the table. The policeman sat down with us. "No, I've had breakfast," he said. But he drank a cup of the coffee mixture my mother had made - a few real coffee beans and mostly "Ersatzkaffee," made of roasted grains. We hardly ever were able to buy real coffee. Sometimes, after a very bad air attack, the Nazi government would try to encourage loyalty by distributing extra rations. On such occasions, we might be able to get a quarter pound of real coffee.

My father wanted to know the reason for the arrest and the trip downtown. "I don't know," the policeman answered. "They called me late last night and told me to bring you in. They never tell me why I am supposed to do anything. I have no idea what they are doing. But, I guess, they have their reasons." He seemed resigned to the way things were.

He drank another sip of our coffee. "Better than the coffee I had earlier!" he volunteered.

Both of them left. I had to go to school. I think my mother was crying at the time I was leaving.

When I came home several hours later, she seemed a bit calmer. But she dropped a plate onto the terrazzo floor in the kitchen. There were little bits of porcelain everywhere. I tried to make her feel better. "I am sure daddy will be back soon." I looked into her face. She tried to smile a little, but again there were tears in her eyes. For a minute, she held me tightly in her arms.

"Didn't you want to finish that picture you were drawing

for daddy?" she asked. And when I nodded she added, "Why don't you do that. He will be so happy to see it .... when he comes back." I believe she nearly said "if" instead of "when." But I went into my room and worked on the picture. I wanted to make sure that it would be the best drawing I had ever attempted.

This time my father did come back. It was about five in the afternoon. As he came through the door, my mother ran into his arms. Now she was really crying. I stood nearby, but I left them alone. I felt relieved. Everything would be good now.

Then we sat in the living room. My parents opened one of the few remaining bottles of champagne that they had reserved for special occasions. There were two or three more bottles down in our basement. My mother had put some baking soda into a glass of juice for me so I would have something that sparkled too. And then my father told us what had happened.

First, they had made him stand in a hallway at the Gestapo, the Nazi secret police headquarters. For three hours he stood. Finally, he was called into one of the rooms. Even then he was not allowed to sit. A rather unfriendly man in uniform had asked him questions about name, date of birth, address, family. Afterwards he was sent back out into the hallway to stand for another two hours. Finally, he was called again. They asked only one question: "Mr. Streufert, what are your personal views about our National Socialist (Nazi) government of Germany?"

Of course, the Gestapo people knew quite well that my father had been fighting the Nazis prior to their final takeover. They did not know about his activities in the underground movement that was trying to remove them from power. Nonetheless, they were quite sure that he had remained hostile to their regime. Would he admit his antagonism and provide them with an obvious reason to arrest and kill him? Or would he be untrue to his beliefs and declare allegiance to the present government?

He did neither. In effect, he managed to trick them.

The Nazis, of course, insisted that their government was perfectly legal. They claimed that they had won a huge majority in the last elections in Germany, although my father knew that the count was, in large part, fraudulent. We had just recently spoken about it. Our family had fled from Berlin, where we had lived while my father was a Senator. We moved to this small town, a suburb of Kiel, for very good reasons. It was a town of people who had worked hard in the shipyards, people who had become foremen and had built their little houses. Most of the residents were staunch socialists and had been members of the now forbidden unions. Some of them had even been communists. My father felt safer among such people. They hated the Nazis as much as he did.

Following that last election, when the Nazis had claimed a 98% majority for Hitler, some brown shirts had paraded through our suburb town, insisting that there had been no more than three votes against their party. "Those three should be shot on the spot!" one of them said. My father had told me, "Maybe there were three votes **for** the Nazis. Maybe even a few more. But their argument that only three people voted against the Nazi party, that is proof of pure fraud!"

With such thoughts in mind, he had an ingenious way to respond to their dangerous question. "Well, gentlemen," he answered the Gestapo inquisitors, "You have announced that your party won the last election with a great majority. You know that I have always believed in democracy. If your announcement of that great victory is accurate, I can hardly object, can I?"

Apparently the Gestapo inquisitor did not know how to deal with the answer. My father was allowed to go home. At least this time.

FIGHTING THE NAZIS

I knew that the Nazis did not trust our family. I knew that we had to be very careful. I was vaguely aware that my father was somehow involved in the underground movement and that the Nazis did not know about those activities. At least not yet. If they had no proof that we were against them, why were we in danger? I wanted to know. One evening I asked my parents.

My father thought for a minute, probably trying to determine how he should answer such a question from a child. "If someone forced you to do things that you don't want to do, things you think are wrong, would you like that person?"

The answer came easily. "Of course not!"

"Well," he continued, "the Nazis are forcing us and a lot of other people to live in a way that we hate. They make us participate in a war that we did not want. They do not allow us to say the things we want to say. We don't like that. We don't like what they are doing to us. Consequently, we do not like them. Surely they can figure out that we are not happy with what they are doing. They know that we would like to live in a very different world; they can guess that we are not pleased with their government. And if we are unhappy with their government, we might want to throw them out. They don't know whether we might think of a way to do that. Of course they don't want to be thrown out of the government. They want to continue to run this country. So they don't trust us."

Throwing them out was something I had not thought of. How could that be possible? They were the government! And how could they know that we would want to throw them out? "But they can't be sure that we are against them!"

"No, they can't be sure. That's why they keep searching our house. That is why they question me from time to time," my father continued. "They think they might find some evidence that would confirm their suspicions."

"But if they cannot be sure, they cannot do anything to really hurt us!" I countered.

"In many countries that is true, most of the time. But it

is not true in Germany today. They do whatever they want. Let me tell you about some things that happened a long time ago, when you were not even born yet."

His face turned thoughtful. The blue eyes seemed to seek the distant past. "It was just a few days before the Nazi takeover. I was meeting with some friends in Stralsund in Pomerania, the area from which I had been elected to the Reichstag (the German parliament). My friends and I had been fighting the Nazis for some time. Right then we were making emergency plans to counter their next move. One of my good friends who lived close to my house had to leave early. Usually he and I walked home together from these meetings. But we were not quite finished with the meeting when he had to leave. I stayed back."

"When our meeting was finally done," he continued, "I started to go home too. A man I knew as a Nazi suddenly walked up to me and said: 'Don't walk home through the forest tonight. They are waiting for you there. You know, I don't approve of that kind of thing.' I did not get a chance to ask him any questions, he disappeared as quickly as he had shown up. So I took a different way home. My friend was not so lucky. They had shot and killed him in that forest. The 'murder' was supposedly investigated, but since the Nazis took power a couple of days later, nobody was ever charged with the crime. What all that means is that they don't need evidence to kill someone. It is enough if they don't like someone or if they distrust that person - and it is even worse if they think he or she might be planning something against them."

"They don't know whether you are planning anything," I objected.

"No, they don't. But they know that I used to do it before they took power. And they suspect that I would still do it if I could."

My mother had come into the room and had heard the last few words. She added, "When the Nazis had big rallies before 1933, they would always ask whether someone wanted to comment on the speech they had given. Daddy used to come forward. He would say only a few sentences that would make the people at the rally laugh at things the Nazi had said. It would

66

make the Nazis furious. That is why they hate daddy. That is why he was declared an 'Enemy of the State' and fired from any and all jobs when the Nazis took power."

My father explained. "An enemy of the state to them really means an enemy of their state. As long as they view us as their enemies, we can expect them to distrust us. Probably as long as they will remain in power."

"Then why don't we just leave? Why don't we go to another country?" I did not like my own question. I did not really want to leave the town where I had grown up. But if it had to be....

"No, we are not leaving!" my father's voice was very firm. "Other people have left, like Thomas Mann, the writer. Now he talks to us from England and tells us to rise up against the Nazis. If he wants to fight the Nazis, why did he not stay here and help? We are staying here. We will do whatever we can to destroy the Nazi regime from inside of Germany. To leave would be cowardly. Besides, we could not leave if we wanted to. The Nazi government would not give us a passport. And during a war it is just about impossible to go anywhere else. We would have to leave for a neutral country - and which country would want Germans now? But that is not the point. We will stay here. We will fight them here!"

I was glad we were staying. I would have missed my home town. I would have missed my friend Friedrich-Karl. But my father's words scared me a bit. There were only three of us and so many more of them!

THE VIEW FROM A SHAKY TREE

It was one of those rare hot summer days. You could see the heat rise from the small granite stones that paved the main road between Kiel and Lübeck. The air above the street appeared to vibrate a little. Distant houses and trees lost their sharp contours. On such a day I could not stay at home. With nothing specific to do, with no plans in mind, I walked very slowly down the road. Near the restaurant "Rosenheim" I ran into two older boys. Normally they would ignore me. To them I was only "a kid." But this time, it was different. "Come!" they called to me. "There are four boys from the other side of town who are after us. They want to beat us up. We need your help. It is really important - and it is lots of fun too!"

"Why are they after you?" I wanted to know.

"It is only a game. But if they catch us, they will beat us up!"

The beating part did not seem reasonable to me. But, at the moment, I had nothing else to do. I thought, "I'll go along with it for a while. Whenever I can think of something better, I will just leave."

"Where are those others?"

"That's just the problem. We don't know for sure. But they could be somewhere close by. And we have got to find out where they are. If we don't, we can't get away from them."

It turned out that the four "enemies" were yet a bit older than the two who had involved me in their game. And, so I was told, the others had binoculars. They would be able to see us from far away.

I asked whether my two associates had seen those four boys any time recently. They had. About half an hour ago, they had been standing on a meadow, about half a mile away from the Rosenheim restaurant. But neither could guess where they might be now.

"But they are sure to come after us!" one of my new companions insisted.

We were standing at the intersection of two main roads, next to the restaurant. Trees and the building kept us from

68

seeing anything in the distance. We could easily have been surprised by our opponents. It was absolutely necessary to get a better view of the area.

One of the roads, the one that led to the Baltic Sea about 30 miles away, turned north next to the Rosenheim and continued downhill towards the river about a mile away. On one side of that road, just beyond the restaurant, stood a tall tree with branches that reached all the way to the ground. I had climbed this tree once, about half-way to the top. It had been easy, so I suggested that we might get a better view from somewhere on that tree.

My suggestion produced enthusiastic agreement. All of us climbed upward - I was ahead of the other two. But there were many leaves on the many branches, so we could hardly see anything at all. An occasional glimpse here and there. But without a panoramic view the search would not yield reliable results. Too bad, - in winter it would have been easy to see everything, even if we had climbed only part of the tree. - But it was summer.

"We could just hide in the tree," I suggested. "They will not see us up here, even if they pass by below."

But the other boys did not like my suggestion. "That would ruin the game," they agreed with each other.

So we had to climb higher. Once we had reached the three-quarter point, there were a few places where we could look into the distance. Yet other areas around us were still completely obscured by the leaves. We had to climb higher yet. I was still a little ahead of the other two. Finally, I could see everything except for the meadows and fields to our south.

"I don't see anything," I reported, "only a few grown ups."

"They would be coming from that direction!" One of the boys pointed toward the south. It was exactly the direction that was still hidden.

"Well, then we have to climb even higher!"

I looked at the branches above me. The tree stretched about another 15 to 20 feet upwards. But the branches were getting awfully thin. Would they be able to support the three of

69

us?

I had doubts. "I don't know whether it is safe to go up further."

But the other boys did not want to give up. They climbed upwards and closer to me. Since they were older and heavier than I, the top of the tree began to sway.

"Stop!" I yelled at them. "It is not going to work like that. Everything up here will break off. Why don't the two of you climb down a few branches. I will go further up. The top will not hold all three of us."

Apparently they must have realized that my suggestion made sense. They did climb back down, just a few feet. The top of the tree stopped moving. It was my turn.

Very carefully I reached for the next branch. I put one foot on it. Then the next. It moved a bit, but it held. Still not a good view toward the South. Another branch higher. The very next one was too thin, it would not hold. But just above it, there was a heavier one. That would be the one. I managed it. The top of the tree began to sway again. But I was able to stand on the branch. The swaying stopped. And the view toward the South was finally open!

I saw them! They were nearly a mile from us, walking in a westerly direction, away from us! It seemed that they were not at all concerned about where we might be. Probably they forgot all about the 'game.'

"It looks to me as though they are going home!" There was no need to stay up in the tree. "Shall we start down?"

The other two boys were beginning to climb back toward the ground. Carefully and slowly, of course. I looked for the branch below me. No, not that thin one. The next one, that second one would hold me. But as my foot reached for it, the top of the tree moved. My foot shifted too far outward and I missed the foothold. All I could do now was to hold on with both hands. I had to find another foothold. Neither of my feet was touching anything. Then the branch in my right hand was beginning to break. If I only would have been better in gymnastics! But probably that would not have helped either. The branch in my right hand snapped off.

I fell. Branches and leaves were striking my face and my hands. My body was pushed away from the tree trunk. I hit a major branch. I was too numb with fear to know whether it hurt.

It seemed to take forever, yet I did not have time to think what might happen once I hit the ground. I only wondered whether my parents would be angry. Again, leaves hit my face. Branches scratched my arms. The contact with the larger branch had turned me around; I could see the top of the tree above me. I would hit the ground with my back! I heard the other boys screaming.

Then it happened. I felt resistance underneath me. One of the broad branches near the bottom of the tree caught me - my downward movement slowed and slowed. Somehow, the lowest branch dropped me relatively gently into last year's leaves below the tree. It was over.

My heart was beating crazily. A few scratches and a little blood, that was all.

The other two boys had not yet reached the ground. By the time they got there, I had managed to calm myself a bit. "Gee, you two are slowpokes!" I said.

Some game!

THE "FINAL SOLUTION"

The Nazis had always used the Jews as convenient scapegoats. German Jews were blamed for all ills of the country. International Jewry was branded responsible for world-wide economic problems or for the destructive effects of the Versailles treaty that was forced upon Germany after the First World War. The word "Jude" (Jew) was used by the Nazis as just another nasty four letter word. Anyone with a Jewish grandparent was prohibited from joining the Nazi party. Anyone with a Jewish parent was an outcast. Any person who had been categorized as Jewish was ordered to wear a Jewish star on their clothing. And the Jews were slowly disappearing. Where to? Most people did not know. Probably they moved away. Often they disappeared in the middle of the night. Probably they could not stand being persecuted. Maybe they joined their relatives in New York or Chicago or Geneva or somewhere. Somehow, the rumor had gotten out that the Jews were being resettled in occupied areas of Poland or Russia. They would no longer be allowed to live in Germany proper. Maybe some of them had been taken east? But why did they not say goodbye to their friends before they left? Strange.... But then you could not raise any questions about where the Jewish Germans had gone. Such questions were not tolerated by the Nazis.

I did not know what happened to the local Jews. Neither did most of the people in town. My parents knew: they secretly listened to British radio. They were part of the underground movement. But they did not tell me that Jews, Gypsies, homosexuals and so many others that were "unworthy" in the view of Nazi leaders were being exterminated. I could not have heard that information by other means; by the 1940s there were no Jews left in our suburb. But even if there had been, nobody would have dared to talk.

Today we know that this was the time of "Endlösung," the "final solution." The Nazis were going to kill all of the Jewish people, no matter whether they were German citizens or foreigners. Himmler, the head of the SS, had established concentration camps that were designed to be "Vernichtungslager," equipped with special facilities that could kill lots of people quickly, effectively, and inexpensively.

I had an uncle, a prominent defense attorney, who was married to a Jewish lady. He was ordered to divorce my aunt. Immediately. There would be no court case. His signature under a document requesting the divorce would be enough. It would be granted automatically because she was Jewish. The Nazis defined it as "racial shame" to have sex with or to be married to a Jewish person. And once he and his wife would be divorced, he was told, the government would take care of her.

He had worked in the justice system long enough. While he did not know for sure, he guessed what their order meant. He loved her. "No!" he told them.

A day later he was disbarred. His office was raided. His house was searched. He had to work as a farm laborer until the war ended. But both he and his wife survived.

SUPPORTING THE WAR EFFORT

My father had been married once before. Harry, his son from that marriage, was some twenty-five years older than I. I liked him, but I felt that he did not visit us often enough. From time to time, he would send me a present. He would manage to find vacuum tubes, despite the scarcity, whenever our Blaupunkt radio would break. Somehow, I knew, that he must be important. And I knew that he did not like the Nazis, that he kept people alive whom the Nazis wanted dead. At the time, I did not know who those people were. I did not find out until the war was over, until the Nazi regime had collapsed.

Harry's problems, just like my father's began in 1933 when the Nazis took power. Harry was in his late twenties at that time. He had actively fought the Nazi movement. As a consequence of those actions, he was fired from his government job.

Wherever he applied for any position that would match his qualifications, he was denied employment. The Nazis had declared him undesirable. Any German company that would hire blacklisted people such as Harry Streufert, especially if they placed such a person into a responsible position, would be in deep trouble. Consequently, he remained unemployed for some time. And since he was fired for political reasons, he could not receive unemployment compensation.

Finally, he found a job as a gate keeper at the Heinkel aircraft factory. Heinkel built, among other airplanes, the HE 111, a two-propeller passenger aircraft, the European competition to the American DC 3. It was an excellent plane that, later on, would be modified into a bomber aircraft.

The Nazis had placed people who were absolutely loyal to their cause into all the departments at the Heinkel factory. Those "spies" were there to listen, to watch, to make sure that no one would dare to work against the Nazi government. Most of these people were not especially competent. Most of them had difficulty doing their jobs. My brother found such a Nazi. He told that man, "You must be important in the company. If there is anything I can do that would help you, let me know. Just give the work to me to do. Most of the time I have nothing to do at that gate house. I could help you."

The Nazi was delighted. Harry did the Nazi's work for some time. Later Harry he suggested, "With all your influence, I am sure you could get me a job inside the company!?" The Nazi could.

Once Harry had been assigned a desk job, he was quickly recognized as an excellent employee. He repeatedly asked to be transferred to other departments. He seemed promising, so his requests were granted. He learned as much as possible about how the company functioned. Then he decided to remain in a department where the boss was about to retire. Soon Harry became department head. Now he interacted directly with Ernst Heinkel, the owner of the company.

Ernst Heinkel, a professor of engineering, loved to design planes. Some people had come to him, suggesting that they could build a new kind of aircraft engine. It would work like a rocket of sorts. It would allow planes to travel faster. A jet engine? It was an unconventional idea. Initially, Heinkel was doubtful. The first tests had not been very successful. But Heinkel was beginning to get fascinated. He wanted to get back into designing. Running a business was not what he wanted to do most. Maybe this young department head, Harry Streufert, maybe he should give that young man more responsibility for the company. That would relieve Heinkel from many administrative duties. Then he could spend more time on aircraft design.....

Harry was agreeable to the suggestion. But the Nazi government was not. They suddenly discovered that the blacklisted Harry Streufert had, without their knowledge, attained a responsible position. Ernst Heinkel received an order from Berlin: "Streufert is to be fired immediately!" But Ernst Heinkel did not heed orders the way many others did. He knew the government needed his expertise and the aircraft his company was building. He shot back: "Do you want me to build planes or not? If you want my planes, leave me alone. I will run the company the way I want to!" The Nazis gave up. They needed his planes. Harry stayed.

One day, as part of the "final solution," the Heinkel Aircraft company received a letter from a Nazi official listing a number of persons who would be "unavailable for work" by a specific date a few weeks later. Their names were Rubinstein, Cohen, and so forth. Harry understood. He went to speak to Heinkel. Together they wrote an urgent letter to the responsible Nazi official, stating that the people on that list were "urgently needed for the war effort" and that "the further construction of aircraft could not proceed without them." The official was forced to give in. The Jewish employees on that list survived.[2]

---

[2] Later on, once the war was over and the Nazi government had collapsed, some of these individuals moved their families to Israel. Harry corresponded with them. During a visit to their old home country, some of them presented him with a picture book of Israel, inscribed with a brief "thank you" note. It reads in part: "..to a true defender of our cause." Harry has since died; the book is now in my possession. A copy of the note is reproduced on the following page.

ISRAEL
With 30 colour plates

There is probably no other country in the world which is as fascinating as Israel. A country of indescribable abundance and poverty alike, it combines the history of a young nation with that of the people who, after living in dispersion for thousands of years, have now once more found their home and their own state independence here.

In a masterly way photographer Arielli has captured the contrasts of this strange country in his 30 colour plates, which depict the landscape and its inhabitants, Israel of today, as well as the surviving traces of a culture that has long since passed into oblivion.

ELKE

There was more than one way to get from our house to my school. Sometimes I would walk along the main street, meeting some of my friends, finally following a small path downhill. For some unknown reason, that path was known to everyone as the "Coffee-Bean Way." I liked chatting with some classmates along Coffee-Bean Way. But on other days, I wanted to be alone. At such times I would take an old unpaved road, past fields and past rows of hedges common in that part of Northern Germany. At first, the road would take me south, mostly downhill. But when I reached the house of the baker, the road turned sharply to the right, traversed a ravine and, after a while, continued past the house where Elke lived. On summer mornings, even before eight o'clock, the time when I had to be in school, I often saw her playing in their front yard.

Elke must have been three or four years old. She seemed to enjoy it when I passed by; she would walk up to the fence and talk to me. Of course, Elke did not tell me anything fascinating. After all, I was about five years older than she. But she was so nice, so full of life! I enjoyed stopping and talking to her, no matter what she had to say. I simply liked her! There were even days when I was disappointed that Elke was not playing in the front yard, that she was not waiting for me to pass by.

Then, one day, I was told that Elke had died. During the evening she suddenly developed a high fever. Our suburb was too small to have its own physician. Most of the medical personnel in nearby towns had been drafted for the military. It was difficult to obtain quick medical aid. Elke had not survived the night.

Now her front yard was empty. No nice, lively little girl! No smiling eyes! No eager talk!

If a bomb had hit Elke's house, I would have understood. Bombs were normal; they were everyday occurrences. Of course people died from bombs! Somehow then I could have accepted her death. I would have been sad, of course. Still, a bomb would have made sense!

But a sudden fever?

WOLFY

Wolfy was a dog, a German Shepherd. Maybe it would be more correct to say that Wolfy **is** a German Shepherd. Of course, dogs do not live as long as human beings. This particular dog was alive when I was a child, some fifty years ago. So how could I possibly suggest that he **is**, not that he **was** a German Shepherd? Well, let me try to explain.

The neighbors who lived to one side of our house were farmers. Theirs was a relatively large farm, with many meadows and fields, some close by - others further away. The family owned many animals - Holstein cows for milk, sheep for wool, horses to pull their wagons, cats to rid the farm of mice and, of course, there was Wolfy. You might think that Wolfy had a real purpose as well. He might have been trained to herd sheep or to drive away thieves. Possibly a watch dog would have been of value to the farmer: during wars, people get hungry. And hungry people may take food that does not belong to them.

But Wolfy did not do anything useful. Despite his breed, a shepherd he was not. Although someone once told me that this dog had caught a thief, I could not believe it. Wolfy liked to be petted by anyone. His bark, at best, meant, "Come and play with me!"

To Wolfy's credit I have to say that he was a purebred. Still he could not have won a medal in a dog show. Not that he was ugly; I always thought of him as a lovely animal. But his back end dragged just a bit, and instead of black and tan he was black and tan and grey. Worse, I don't think that anyone could have persuaded this dog to stand still, to hold his head high, feet placed just right. No, Wolfy would easily have won the Booby Prize in a dog show. He would just droop, flop onto the ground and look soulful. But I did not care. I loved that dog.

I had always wanted to have my own German Shepherd. But my parents would not yield to my desire. After all, we did not have enough to eat for ourselves. How would we possibly have enough to feed a large dog? Our neighbors were farmers. Their harvests provided them with enough to eat, they were able to feed an animal. Wolfy always had enough food.

79

Anyway, I did not get my own dog. But, that did not matter; I had Wolfy. And I believe that Wolfy was just as attached to me as I was to him, even though I was not his registered owner.

Wolfy and I spent many hours meandering across meadows and fields around the town. There were fewer houses then, but there were brooks and ponds, and bushes and trees around the ponds. Yes, and there were wild rabbits and many other animals that Wolfy liked to chase. He never caught them; I am sure that he did not really try to catch them either. It seemed that he only wanted to find out whether he could run as fast as the animal that was trying to escape. Sometimes, running as swiftly as he could, Wolfy would get as close as a yard or two. Then he would slow down and follow the creature for a short distance. Finally, he would just stop, watch the animal run away, and then race back toward me.

When no wild rabbits were around, I would throw large pieces of wood for Wolfy to fetch. He brought them back to me and dropped them at my feet, over and over again. But after all that running, Wolfy would get hot. His pink tongue would hang out of his mouth and his brown soulful eyes would tell me that he needed water. So we would walk to the pond in the middle of a field. There Wolfy could drink. In short, we understood each other well.

I always enjoyed taking the dog with me. It was even more fun when the two of us visited the ram, a three-colored male sheep that had to be kept in a meadow all by himself. The ram would not allow any other animal in "his" space; he would relentlessly attack. But the farmer kept him despite his bad behavior. After all, his fur had great value. He was white, dark-brown and some other in-between color, spotted in different places over his fairly large body. The farmer's wife was very adept at her spinning wheel. After the ram's long fur had been cut in the spring, the wool would be separated by color and spun. The wool threads would soon become pullovers and sweaters, sometimes with brown squares on a white background or some other combination. Surely the war saved the ram from being turned into meat; wool sweaters could no longer be bought in the stores.

As I already suggested, the ram was not very friendly. Yet that was exactly why Wolfy and I would visit him often. He would always attack the two of us. First, the ram would watch us come closer, head slightly lowered, eyes looking upwards toward us. As soon as we had come as close as about 600 feet, he would lower his head still further - and then he would charge. His speed would increase as he came closer, or so it seemed. It was incredibly exciting! I knew I could get out of his way in time, but nonetheless, I could feel a tingling down my spine. It was a kind of fear, but this was a "good" kind of fear. I could hear the trampling of his feet coming closer and closer. My heart would beat faster. Sometimes I thought I could already smell his damp body. He would only be about three of four feet away, and....

Wolfy and I knew what to do. We waited until the last moment. I yelled, "Toro!" and jumped aside. Of course, Wolfy did not say anything. As a rule he got out of the way just a bit sooner than I did. And in winter, when I was wearing a coat, I would take it off and let the coat slide over the ram's body. He would race past us, probably astonished that his head had not touched anything more substantial than my coat. He would slow down, stop and look around. We were still there!

"Oh, that is where they are!" he probably thought - if a ram thinks like that. He would turn around and once more race toward us. This time he would not be as far away and, consequently, could not attain so much speed. Again we would jump aside just as he was about to reach us. And again he would race past. Once more the ram would turn around, bewildered, lower his head and attack. That game would continue for another two minutes or so; the distances between us would get shorter and shorter. I don't know whether the animal would just get tired or, after a while, the distance between him and us would be too short to allow him to initiate another attack. He would give up. He even let me pet him, especially around his neck. Little scratches on top of his head and around his neck seemed to be what he liked most. Still, we had to be careful when we walked away. Sometimes, as we had walked a few hundred feet away, he would attack again.

The many walks with Wolfy were always fun for both of us. When I would come to the farm next door, the dog often tried to persuade me to join him on one of those excursions. He would run toward the next meadow, turn around, yelp a couple of times: "Come with me!" And, whenever I had the time, he got his way. We shared many experiences! We were always good friends!

As I grew up, Wolfy was getting old. He was not able to run anymore. The back end of his body drooped more and more. Most of the time he would just lie in the sunshine. I would come and pet him and he would lick my hand. We still loved each other, even though the time for walking across the meadow and for teasing the ram were a thing of the past.

And then, one day, Wolfy was gone. "He died last night," said the farmer's wife. She nearly cried. She had loved that dog as much as I had.

Soon there was a German Shepherd puppy on the farm. They called him Wolfy as well, but it was not the same. The new dog and I got along well, but we never became close friends. Maybe it was because I missed my old friend so much. But dead is dead. I would never see my Wolfy again!

A couple of months later, I was playing ball with the farmer's son. He wanted to show me something - I don't remember what it was - and I never got to see it anyway. I went with him. But the thing I saw in the living room is something I will never forget. It was Wolfy.

Wolfy was lying on the floor. It was Wolfy's fur - brown and tan and grey. It was lying flat on the floor, like a throw-rug, with glass eyes. I turned away.

I would never walk into that room again.

THIS IS ENGLAND.....

Nazi radio stations did not broadcast reliable information. When German armies were thrown back, somewhere deep inside of Russia, the newscaster would say that the front lines had been "straightened." When hundreds lost their homes during an Allied air attack on Kiel or an attack on other cities, the Nazi radio announcer claimed that the air raid had been "without any success." Any information that listeners might have interpreted as unfavorable was avoided. Nazi propaganda prevailed. But if the Nazi ministry of propaganda under the direction of Josef Göbbels viewed some event as "positive" for the Nazi regime, we got to hear it over and over again.

Quite in contrast, news broadcast in the German language by BBC, the British Broadcasting Corporation, tended to be very reliable. My parents were intent on knowing how the war was going. When would the Nazis be beaten? How much longer would it take? Would we, all of us, survive long enough to witness the end of the Nazi regime?

BBC news provided potential clues. I still remember the signal that would precede news on the British radio: four tympany beats, somewhat similar to the first four notes of Beethoven's fifth symphony. Then the same words, three times in a row: "This is England, this is England, this is England. You are listening to the news."

My father had attached a long antenna wire to a tall birch tree about 30 yards from the house. The wire led toward the house and through the window frame into our large Blaupunkt radio. Whenever a storm would move the tree enough to snap the antenna wire, my father quickly repaired it. Contact with the world outside was important. Without that antenna, short wave reception was very poor and the BBC station was inaudible.

The Nazi government had made it very clear that listening to foreign radio stations was illegal and would be severely punished. My father said, "If they catch us, we will suddenly be less tall, exactly by the size of one head." It was gallows humor. He was talking about the guillotine, the old capital punishment system of the French Revolution. The Nazis had reintroduced it.

They were using it extensively to "reward" all those German citizens who carelessly said something that could have been interpreted as critical of Nazi activities. The same treatment awaited anyone who engaged in even a minor action that was forbidden by Nazi rules. In other words, we had to be very, very careful. But there was a way to be adequately careful and still listen to the British newscasts. My parents would place a heavy blanket over both their heads and the radio. The blanket would muffle the sound. It was necessary. We never knew who might hear.

Once the Nazis had placed a listening device inside the wall of our house. The microphone had been inserted from the outside. During the 1940s, such devices were still relatively crude and large. My father noticed that the wallpaper was bulging. He carefully removed a bit of the paper, cut a lead wire and replaced the wallpaper. From time to time he would check that the device had not been replaced by a new one.

However, we never knew whether there might be another listening device someplace in our house. We never knew whether someone might be listening outside of the window or whether somebody might walk in at the wrong time.

The blanket that covered my parents and the radio was needed to make sure that nobody would hear. They would turn the wavelength selection knob on the Blaupunkt radio to short-wave and the BBC station. Despite the blanket, the volume would be kept as low as possible.

At that same time, I would go outside to "play." Sometimes I would take my soccer ball and bounce it up and down, walking in continuous circles around the house. I was not actually playing with the ball; I was watching everything that was happening. If some other person would walk toward our house, I quickly went inside and tapped my parents on their blanket covered shoulders. They, in turn, would switch the radio back to the Nazi AM station, would fold up the blanket and would act as though they had just listened to a "legitimate" broadcast. Fortunately, one of the Nazi stations was located at just about the same dial position on AM where BBC was located on short wave. Most of the time, a flip of the wavelength switch was enough.

I played this "game" with my ball many times. I invented other reasons to keep circling the house. Generally no one came, and my parents would be able to hear the entire broadcast. Occasionally, I had to interrupt them. But one evening, things got a bit problematic.

As usual, I was bouncing the ball, walking slowly around the house. As I turned one of the corners, our neighbor saw me. The wheat had been harvested on his fields. Now he was shoveling grain from a wooden, horse-drawn wagon into large 100 pound sacks. Yesterday, the threshing machine had been at the farm. It was time to fill the sacks with wheat. Tomorrow the harvest would be taken to the nearby mill.

"Come here!" he called me. "You can help a little." On that evening he did not have anyone to hold the sacks for him. Most of his workers had been drafted to fight in the German armies. His son, an officer in the air force, had just been killed in action. The Russian POWs assigned to his farm were busy elsewhere.

Generally I was glad to help the farmer. He was a fairly nice man, a bit authoritarian perhaps. Most of the time I learned something new whenever he talked with me. But today it would be different.

I could hardly help him and protect my parents at the same time. I thought of an excuse. "I am supposed to come inside - in just a few seconds!" But he was not to be dissuaded. "A few seconds is not now! Just come over here and help." I had no choice.

"Here, hold this sack. No, not like that. I can't put anything into it if you hold it like that." He showed me how to hold the sack, not end to end, but stretching out only part of the opening. That way the rest of the material at the opening would drop downward, providing space for his shovel and the wheat. "That's it!" He smiled at me when I followed his instructions.

The first sack was quickly filled. Then a second. And a third. As he placed the third sack to the side, I noticed an older boy, dressed in a Hitler Youth uniform. He was leaving the neighbor's house and walking toward ours. He carried a small container, the kind that was used to collect coins and bills for a

85

variety of purposes. Possibly "Winter-aid-funds" or some other officially sanctioned cause. We never believed that the money would be used for beneficial causes. Probably they were just adding money to the war effort. Young people in Nazi uniform kept coming to collect money with increasing frequency.

The Hitler Youth was getting closer to our house. I had to go and warn my parents! Our front door, as always, would not be locked. The kid could might the door bell and wait. But he could just as well walk in and catch them! I had to go and warn them!

"I have to go now!"

But the farmer did not want me to leave. "Your parents won't mind," he insisted, "I will tell them why you stayed here. And when they really want you to come inside, they will come looking for you. Just hold that sack open!" This one was now about two-thirds full.

I held on. He filled it and put it aside. The youth was closer. The farmer took another sack. "Hold this one! And look at what you are doing. You are not holding it right!" His authoritarian nature began to limit his tendency to be friendly with children. Shovel after shovel of grain. As that sack was a bit more than half full, the Hitler Youth was heading directly for our front door. He was no more than fifty feet away. I dropped the sack. The wheat poured onto the dirt. I raced toward the house, slammed the door behind me and tapped on my parents' shoulders. The doorbell rang. The blanket flew aside. The switch on the radio jumped to AM. Nazi news was coming from the speaker.

My parents went to the front door. I stayed. I was shaking. The brown-shirted Youth and the farmer were both at our front door. The Youth wanted money. The farmer was furious.

"Siegfried is usually very nice and helpful," the farmer complained. "But this time he poured a whole sack of grain onto the ground. It was pure and simple nastiness! He did not want to help me and decided to get back at me for asking him to stay! He must be punished for that kind of stupid behavior! Such things should not happen! And at a time when people are starving all over this country! Wheat is so scarce!"

I was afraid. What would happen now? But I had no choice! After all, I had to warn my parents!

I felt a little better when my father's voice remained calm. "We will take care of it. Siegfried will be treated appropriately. And I am very sorry about the spilled grain. Can I help you to pick it up?"

"No!" The farmer shook his head vehemently. "That wheat is wasted. The chickens will eat it." He walked away.

My parents gave a few pennies to the Hitler Youth, about as little as they could get away with.

I heard their steps coming toward the room. I was sitting on the sofa, pressed into a corner. What would happen now? I must have looked rather pale as they walked in. My mother was first through the door and put her arms around me. And my father came and stroked my hair. "Thank you!" He smiled at me. "You did that well!"

KID SPIES

One day, our teacher spent the morning talking to all four grades in our classroom. It was an unusual event - typically he taught only one grade at a time while the rest of us had to work on some assigned task. Not today. We should listen carefully, he insisted. He had something very important to tell us!

He began by glorifying Hitler and his "victories." He spent much time explaining how the Nazi government had "saved Germany from ruin."

"But you know all about that." He continued, "I have told you about Hitler and his great deeds many times. You know about the fabulous future of our country under Hitler's leadership. You know that the National Socialist (Nazi) party is determined to make every German happy. You know that we will win the war against anyone who dares to stand in our way!"

"But some of your parents have not had the opportunity to learn as much as you have. Of course, it is not their fault. They don't go to school any more. They can't hear what I am telling you!"

He looked at us intently. "You must help them," he said very seriously. "If your parents say that they don't like Adolf Hitler or the party, if they ever mention that they don't feel good about our government, you should tell me right away! If your parents don't like the war, I need to know. Tell me all the things your parents have said. That way I will know what kind of mistake they are making. That way we will know what to teach them. You see, I want to make sure that your parents understand everything as well as all of you do!"

He was silent for a moment to let the message sink in. He looked around the classroom. "Is there any one of you who wants to tell me something right now?"

Not one child raised a hand. The teacher seemed disappointed. Again he urged us to speak. Nobody did.

"Well, you don't have to talk about it now. Not in front of all the other students. Come to me after school is over. Remember, I want to help your parents. Make sure to tell me everything you have heard!"

It was hardly surprising that none of us volunteered our parents' views. Most children had no idea how adults in their world felt. Only kids whose parents had accepted the Nazi point of view had heard their parents speak about politics. Any adult who disagreed was very quiet about it. Such things could not be discussed in front of children. Children might inadvertently repeat something their parents said. Disagreement with Nazi actions or doubts about their policies could not even be discussed in front of other adults. Even "friends" might be Nazi spies. Just repeating a rumor that might imply something negative about the government or the Nazi party could land one in jail or worse. It was much too dangerous to speak to anyone, unless one absolutely knew that this person was anti-Nazi. And, if you did know someone to whom you could speak freely, you had to do it far away from possible listeners - somewhere deep in a forest, or quietly at night in a bedroom.

The Nazis had established a very effective system of information control. Listening to anything other than Nazi radio stations was severely punished. Literature or newspapers with differing views were forbidden and unavailable. Communication among the population, except for statements that supported the Nazis, was carefully controlled. Nazi propaganda glorified the successes of the system and ignored its failures. Government actions which the general population might have considered objectionable were kept under tight cover. By controlling information, by generating a fear of severe punishment for obtaining and communicating "illegal" information, the Nazis assured that the majority of Germans were kept ignorant. Information is power. Absence of information generates weakness.

Indeed, it was risky to tell a child anything that contrasted with the "standard" Nazi line. Nonetheless, my parents spoke to me about their views even when I was only a small child. Somehow, for some reason, they must have decided to confide in me. Possibly they were afraid that they might not survive Nazi persecution; that they had to train me to understand their views while they were still alive. Possibly they felt that I would never

89

be able to reach my own conclusions if I would not be exposed to varied points of view. Whatever their rationale might have been, I knew about their views - and somehow I had learned to keep those views secret.

Of course I would not tell the teacher about my parents' attitudes. Any information that they did not support the Nazis would have amounted to a death sentence for them. I **knew** they would be taken away and killed. For me, it could also mean death or, more likely, full-time residence in a Nazi school.

NATIONAL POLITICAL EDUCATION

Not far from Kiel, the Nazis had established a school for future leaders of their cause - The National Political Education Institution at the castle in Plön. Candidates for this school were carefully selected on the basis of intellectual competence. Local Nazi leaders could recommend a child as a potential student. If accepted, the child would live at the castle and would receive extensive physical and political training.

The local Nazi leader in our town decided to recommend my friend Friedrich-Karl. He had not discussed this action with Friedrich-Karl's parents. They did not find out until their son had already been accepted. Then the Nazi leader came to their house and informed them that their son would be trained for future Nazi leadership. He emphasized that they had no choice in the matter: Friedrich-Karl was going!

My friend tried to refuse. His resistance only generated anger. The Nazi insisted. My friend was to appear at the appropriate time and at the appropriate place as commanded.

At the castle in Plön, he was placed in a class with others of the same age. Their mornings were spent on sports, sprinting and other physical activities. In the afternoon they were taught some normal school subjects, but everything was tainted with Nazi propaganda. Much time was spent discussing the life of Adolf Hitler.

Friedrich-Karl decided to get out any way he could. Of course, he knew he would not be released if he requested it. Rather, he had to make sure they would send him home on their own volition. His strategy was straightforward. He did not participate in discussions. In fact, he did not say a word. When, after a couple of days, the children were tested in a number of subjects, he intentionally responded incorrectly to most of the questions.

The political authorities at the school concluded that the Nazi leader of our town had made a serious mistake. Obviously, Friedrich-Karl was not sufficiently competent to become a Nazi leader. In fact, by their measure, this kid was not competent in anything at all!

Friedrich-Karl was sent home. It was time for him and his parents to celebrate. Quietly, of course.

RATS

Somewhat back of our house stood an old barn. Once upon a time, it had been the most important part of the farm next door. In later years, the farmer had built a huge new barn attached to a large building that housed the animals. This new building, in turn, was connected to their substantial home.

Nonetheless, the old barn was still in use. In a large room on the left they kept pigs. The grunting of those creatures was clearly audible whenever anyone approached the building. On the right they raised calves; on the upper level, straw, hay and some grain were stored. The farmer had given us some space on the upper level where we could store potatoes and whatever vegetables and other foodstuffs we wanted to keep for the winter.

But there was a problem with storing food in the barn - rats. We tried everything to get rid of those pests: poison, traps, even the temporary storage of grain elsewhere. Nothing helped. Sure a few rats had been destroyed. But there were always enough others to take their place. And if the grain was removed, the rats would merely come downstairs and enjoy the pig food.

One of the Russian POWs who was assigned to work for the farmer suggested that we should catch a rat and singe its tail. That rat would then tell the others about the miserable experience. They would all move out.

"It worked at home in Russia!" he insisted.

Supposedly he caught a couple of animals alive and twice released a rat with a singed tail. But the German rats did not cooperate. They stayed and multiplied.

Among other things, we had stored a bag of noodles just above the steps in the old barn. We had wrapped the noodles well and, in addition, had placed them in a heavy cardboard container to protect them from rodents. One morning, my mother asked me to fetch a few. I walked up the old wooden steps to the upper level. I surprised a rat which had just managed to tear open the container where our food was kept. I was furious!

I don't know whether the animal failed to notice my

arrival or whether it was just incredibly unafraid. I backed off slowly and walked gently down the steps in search of a weapon. There - a pitchfork! That should do! Carefully and quietly I went back upstairs.

The rat was still chewing on our noodles. That animal was clearly very fat. "That beast is not hungry," I thought, "and all of us **are** hungry. And it is eating our food!" I slowly moved closer. The rat heard me. It stopped chewing, turned its head and looked. But it must have enjoyed its morning meal too much; it turned back to the noodles and continued eating. Now I stood on the uppermost step, lifted the pitchfork above my head, tensed my muscles and aimed. The pitchfork came down hard. The animal squeaked, ran left, then turned to the right, trying to reach the steps where I was standing. But I was faster. The pitchfork was up again and once more crashed onto the rat. It was no longer able to move as well as before. But it tumbled down three steps and tried to continue downward. Now I stood above it. I lifted the pitchfork and, this time, used it as a dagger.

Red blood flowed from the wound. The rat jerked a couple of times, then it lay still. I felt sick and turned away. But I had to look at the bleeding dead animal again as I walked down the steps.

What had I done? Was that torture? Should I simply have chased the creature away? But it was fat; it was eating our food - and we did not have enough to eat! After passing the rat I stood on the steps below it for a while, never looking upwards. Somehow I had lost my orientation.

The farmer walked in. He saw me with the pitchfork. Then he saw the dead rat.

"Did you kill it?" he wanted to know. I nodded.

"Good job! Keep that up!"

I was not so sure that it had been a good job. One thing was certain. I would not keep it up.

ARREST

August 1944.   Someone was pounding on the door and ringing the doorbell.   It was about five in the morning. We had been sleeping.

We all knew the meaning of the early morning hour and the serious demeanor of the policeman. This was serious. Only a couple of weeks ago, there had been an attempt on Hitler's life. Military officers, politicians and members of the intelligentsia had united to try to kill him. They had failed. But the Nazis were scared.

It was not likely that someone had obtained information about my father's association with the underground movement. But even without such knowledge, his past as a Senator of the Social Democratic Party and his early activities against the Nazi movement during the late 1920s and early 30s made him a suspect.

Once more I was scared. I hid in my parents' bedroom and did not want to leave. I heard the policeman's boots in the hallway. He was following my father, step by step. There was no time for breakfast. "We have to be there before six-thirty," the uniformed man announced.

The policeman was kind enough to allow my parents to say a private goodbye in the bedroom. For a minute they were alone, except for me. We all put our arms around each other.

My father looked at the open window. It would have been simple for him to jump out. It would have been so simple to disappear. They never would have found him - he had enough connections in the underground.

He looked at the window.   Then he looked at my mother. And at me. No, he would not risk his family. He knew that the Nazis would avenge his disappearance. If he were gone, they would arrest and possibly torture or kill his wife and child. Once more he kissed my mother and returned to the hallway where the policeman was waiting. They left.

My mother was pale. In a way, she looked almost dead.

I was still afraid. "Should we hide?" I asked. She tried to calm my fears, "We must be here when Daddy comes back."

I waited. He was not back when I came home from school. I waited all evening. Finally, it was time to go to sleep. I promised myself that I would wake up if the doorbell rang. It never did.

DRAGON LAKE

He did not come back the following day. Nor the next. My mother took the train to downtown Kiel and inquired at the state offices of the NSDAP, the Nazi Party. I stayed at home. When she came back, she told me that she had to wait a long time before anyone would speak with her. They sent her to the headquarters of the secret police, the Gestapo. There they interrogated her. Finally, she was allowed to tell them why she came: she wanted information about my father's fate. She was told that he had been placed into the Concentration Camp "Dragon Lake." Yes, she could get a visitor's pass. However, such a pass would be issued only if there were important non-personal reasons for a visit. For example, she could see him once if she and my father had to resolve financial matters. But there would only be one visit. Never any more.

She obtained a visitor's pass for the next Thursday. "You must leave now," the official ordered after issuing the pass. "Heil Hitler."

There was nothing more my mother could have done. Security systems were everywhere. Armed men in Nazi uniform stood close by. If she had not left, she too would have disappeared. That she could not risk. There was still a child to raise and she could hope that the war would end soon. She could hope that the Nazi regime might soon collapse. Considering the state of the war, it could not last much longer. Maybe not even a year.....

When Thursday came, I wanted to go with her to Dragon Lake. It seemed such an appropriate name! But I was not allowed to go. The visitor's pass was registered to my mother alone. I had to stay at home. I waited and waited for her return. What would she have seen? What would she tell me? What was a concentration camp? I asked my friends in school. I asked my best friend's parents after school. Nobody knew of such a thing. "A concentration camp? Are you sure you got that name right? Maybe it is something new...."

My mother returned in the late afternoon. She had been allowed to speak with my father for fifteen minutes. The conversation with him had had a major emotional impact on her. The sights she had seen at the Dragon Lake camp seemed to have changed her. She told me of the guards with submachine guns. She spoke of the careful attention those guards paid to anything that was said, to any slight movement. It looked as though they were ready to aim and fire their guns immediately; they seemed quite willing to kill anyone who might say or do something that would displease them. And she told me about the inmates she saw, scared and skinny, held back by electrified barbed wire.

As she left the camp, she was told that it was forbidden to mention the existence of this concentration camp to anyone. Providing information about anything she had seen would be considered "treason" and would be punished by death. She was told that, "This installation is a secret operation for the protection of the country."

Upon leaving, she was supposed to turn in her visitor's pass. But the concentration camp guard at the gate said, "Why don't you keep it. It is issued for Thursday. There is no date. Come back next week - you can see your husband again." My mother thanked him. What strange kindness in the middle of that vicious horror...."

She repeated her trip to Dragon Lake the following week. But my father was no longer there. "Gone," said the administrator. "He was sent somewhere else. You have to leave now. Heil Hitler."

"But where was he sent?"

The answer was curt: "We cannot provide any information."

Yet, as my mother was leaving, one of the guards handed her a small torn piece of wrapping paper. "From your husband."

After leaving the camp she read:

"My love,

I am sorry that we cannot see each other again. Try everything to attain my freedom. I cannot do anything from where I am or will be. I don't know where they are sending us. Please keep our love alive - and thank you for all the wonderful things you have done. Have courage, God will be with us. All my love and kisses to you and to our son."

CAPTAIN HERTEL

My mother had been thinking about people she knew, anyone who might be able to help. Was there anyone with some degree of influence, some amount of power, who might be able to help free my father? One person who came to mind that autumn was Captain Hertel, a tall, greying captain in the German Navy. In the past, he had commanded his own ship. He was injured when his ship was sunk. The vessel was torpedoed close to German shores. Nobody knew for certain which nation's submarine had gotten that close.

As a result of his injury, Mr. Hertel was limping. Duty at sea was no longer possible. Recently he had been assigned to an office in the high command of the German Navy, a large building a bit north of downtown. Despite all the destruction in Kiel, the navy command had not been hit. We often saw Captain Hertel walking past our house early in the morning and late in the evening, always dressed in full navy uniform. Everyday he would ride the train to and from work in the city - that is, whenever the train tracks had not been damaged by some recent air attack. Our house was located between the train station and his home and I often waved to him as he walked by.

Mr. Hertel seemed a nice man. He would always smile and wave back. I liked his blue uniform, it was so much more attractive than anything the other military services were wearing. Most of all, it was so much more attractive than all the brown Nazi shirts.

We had known Mr. and Mrs. Hertel for some time, not very well, but enough to chat occasionally. He once spent a few hours in our basement when an air attack began just as he was passing by. We had talked a bit then, and my mother knew that the navy captain was not an enthusiastic supporter of the Nazi regime. So when Captain Hertel passed our house one evening, my mother asked whether he might be able to speak with her for a couple of minutes. "Sure," he said.

My mother reported what had happened to my father. He had not heard, yet he did not seem especially surprised. As she told him about the arrest and about Dragon Lake, his forehead creased and his eyes began to look angry.

"Bastards! They are destroying this country! They got us into a stupid war that we cannot win. And now they are taking our best people and locking them up. They are lower class bums, just fanatics that have no idea what they are doing!"

"Is there anything that I should do? Can you suggest anything? Can you possibly help in any way?" my mother wanted to know.

"There isn't much anybody can do...." Captain Hertel was slowly shaking his head. "They've gotten too much control. They listen to everything we do in Navy Command. They control us all. We are just like puppets - and they pull the strings. You saw what happened when the military and the intelligentsia rose up against Hitler. Do you think Field Marshall Rommel was killed in action, as they say? No, they killed him. And they will kill anyone who disagrees with them!"

His voice was quieter now, more thoughtful. "You must deal with them directly. You have to make them believe that your husband is not dangerous to their regime. I will be glad to write a letter on his behalf. But that is all I can do. It will probably do no good. The Nazis don't like the military. They don't trust us, for good reason. They are in a world by themselves."

My mother's brown eyes began to look grey. Another bit of hope was vanishing. "Can't someone, can't the military end this war?"

He smiled a little, but it looked like a smile of resigned desperation. "We in the Navy, right here in Kiel, stopped the First World War. But we can't do it this time. We can't even talk to each other without their listening to everything that we are saying. They have listening devices and spies everywhere. One of my fellow officers said something a bit critical last winter. It was not very negative, just doubtful. He said it among other officers. The next day he did not come to work. We had no idea what happened. Then an obituary appeared in the paper. Killed in combat. He got a very large obituary statement. A lot of good that did him. He was not killed in combat. The Nazis got him!"

"No, there is not much we can do if we can't even talk

to each other. I don't think that Germany can win this war. We don't have the manpower or the weapons to fight the whole world. I wish we could stop the nonsense. But even if we could throw the bastards out, I don't think the British, the Americans or the Russians would stop fighting now, even if we asked for a cease-fire. It is too late. They know they are winning. They know that we can't last much longer."

He got up to go. "My thoughts and my feelings are with you, Mrs. Streufert." He smiled a little. "Try the direct route. Go to the national party leadership. They <u>can</u> do something - <u>if</u> they want to. And," he added with another one of his terse resigned smiles, "of course we will keep quiet about what both of us said tonight. I do hope your husband will be back soon. He is a good man. I liked him." The past tense sounded ominous.

At the door he turned one more time. "Take care. And don't give up, no matter what. Somehow, some way, some time we will yet save this country. Good night."

Sure, our country, Germany, was important to us. Getting rid of the Nazis was very important. But somehow, at the moment, the most important thing was getting my father back. That was the foremost concern, especially for my mother.

MR. JANSEN

I understood what the Nazis were about. My parents had often talked about them, about their views and their intents. I knew that some of them were truly nasty people. But I also knew that some among them were only misguided. They wanted to be nice people, but they had become true believers in a cause that was not nice.

One individual who had probably joined the Nazi Party in blind belief was Mr. Jansen. He had lived through the poverty and the starvation in Germany during the 1920s. He had experienced the inflation that caused a loaf of bread to cost billions of Marks. He had suffered from the turmoil that followed the First World War and the disastrous impact of the Versailles Treaty. He saw the foundation of the German economy carted away as "reparations" to other countries. And he had concluded that something needed to be done.

The Nazi party had promised an end to the tragedy. And after the Nazis took power, the economy did initially improve. Mr Jansen became an enthusiastic supporter. To him, the Nazis were right. They would be, he thought, the salvation of the country. They would stop people from starving. They would make Germany a great place to live. He would be one of them. He not only joined the party, he was soon elected to lead that party in our town. He wanted to do whatever he could to improve the life of the local population. He believed that Nazi policies would do just that.

I am not sure when and where my parents met Mr. Jansen. He and his wife were always nice to us, even though my father's past activities were entered into the local party's "enemies of the state" records. We gave the Jansens strawberries from our garden, they brought us apples from theirs. When we met on the street, I would greet them with "Good Morning," or whatever the time of day suggested. Neither my parents nor I would use the obligatory "Heil Hitler." The Jansens would also respond with "Good Morning." They were not fanatics.

Mr. Jansen worked somewhere in Kiel. When he was home during weekends, he would spend much time in his basement. The walls in the basement held an incredible number of tools. He built wonderful items from wood: furniture, utensils of various kinds and,... toys. Sometimes he would build things for me, among them very detailed wooden toy cars. I was delighted. After all, during the war toys could not be bought in stores. And sometimes Mr. Jansen would teach me how to use some of his tools. I had a small chest with kid-size tools at home, but nothing like these!

A couple of years into the war Mr. Jansen resigned as local leader of the Nazi party. I do not know whether he asked to be relieved of his duties or whether he was forced out. Someone else, a younger man, a firebrand with a desire for prominence, became the local party leader.

When Mr. Jansen heard about my father's arrest, he did everything he could to obtain his release. He called party officials. He wrote a very positive report about my father and turned it into the county offices. The county chief of the Nazi party demanded that he withdraw the report. Mr. Jansen refused. He wrote several more letters. He traveled to the state offices in Kiel to personally appeal to the authorities. Nothing worked.

Finally, he gave up. "I am afraid there is not much we can do," he concluded sadly. "The order to arrest your husband must have come from far above. The state level of the party has no control. And once someone has been arrested on order of some central national authority, it is typically too late to do anything. We will just have to wait until they decide to set him free."

In the meantime, Mr. Jansen and his wife did whatever they could to make life easier for my mother and myself. One time he carved four sailboats for me. His wife made the sails. He fastened the boats on boards that were attached to each other in the form of a cross. One boat was sailing east, another north, the third west and the last south. Then he mounted the cross with the boats perpendicular to a vertical post. The cross with the boats rested on a steel rod that extended from the post, allowing the boats move with the wind. Now the boats could sail; they could turn around each other whenever the wind was blowing. I loved the beautiful toy.

I dug a hole for the post in front of my window. Often I dreamily watched the circular sailing of my boats. And I was looking forward to the day when I could show that wonderful present to my father. Yes, I would show it to him as soon as he was back with us.

FIRE! - IN MINIATURE

People who must cope with dangerous and scary situations on a day-to-day basis can either try to run and hide or they can try to cope by understanding the danger to the degree possible. Attempts to cope are often evident when experiences are potentially life threatening. The "games" we "played" with fire are a good example.

Air raid alarms had long become routine. During the day, the attackers continued to be American planes; at night, it was the British. Sometimes both would show up during the same twenty-four hour period. On certain days Kiel was the target on two or three separate occasions. Our suburban town lost more and more homes and farm buildings to the bombs. More and more houses burned down. The straw-thatched roofs that had dominated the town were slowly disappearing.

All of us knew that someday it would be our turn. Someday we would not be able to extinguish the incendiary bombs that continued to hit our houses. Someday our homes would burn down. Would we be able to save ourselves? If my best friend's house burned down, would he be able to get out? If my parents' house went up in flames, how would I best survive? We talked about it. Friedrich-Karl and I wanted to know.

The two of us constructed several miniature houses, some smaller, some larger. We used bricks for the exterior and interior walls. There were enough old bricks around. We picked them up from the piles of rubble that remained when neighbors' houses were destroyed by bombs. Three or four bricks, stacked on top of each other, were enough to represent the walls. We left spaces for windows and doors. After we had carefully copied the rooms and hallways in the interior of our real homes, we filled some of the rooms with hay or straw. Dried grass would do too. It represented the flammable materials found in houses, for example furniture, clothing, interior doors, and so forth. Where a room might be especially prone to burn, we would even add a little gasoline, if it was available. Finally, we would build the roof of plywood or some other kind of wooden board that we had found in the rubble. The house was finished.

Now we would throw a match into the house - sometimes in one place, at other times in another. After all, it was impossible to predict where an incendiary bomb might hit and where the fire would start.

It is burning! We watched the spreading fire very carefully.

"If the bombs hit the living room, you can't get out in the front of the house!"

"But the back door is still safe. Or that window on the other side!"

"I am not sure! The smoke is drifting that way. You would not be able to breathe! Look how fast the fire is spreading! If we were in the basement, would we have gotten out?"

"I think so, but only if we knew right away that the fire had started. Otherwise it would be too late."

"There should be a direct exit from the basement to the outside. Look at that! I wouldn't want to be upstairs, though. We would never escape from there!"

Whether these quasi-scientific investigations would have helped us to survive a real fire remains uncertain. Fortunately our houses did not burn down. Both our homes were repeatedly hit by incendiary bombs, but our parents were either able to extinguish the fires or to pick the bomb canisters up with a shovel and throw them outside. Fortunately, our houses did not burn down. But Friedrich-Karl's house was severely damaged when a bomb exploded only a few yards away. The entire rear wall of the house was gone!

"My love,   Neuengamme, Sept. 19, 1944
    I am well........"

Finally, we received a letter from my father. He had been transported to a concentration camp near Hamburg, the camp Neuengamme. Twice a month concentration camp inmates were allowed to write a letter up to 16 lines long. Each letter had to include a statement indicating that the inmate felt fine. The letters were censored by the guards. Any letter that contained suspicious statements or did not conform to stringent instructions was destroyed. The printed letterhead differed slightly from time to time, but the information it contained was basically the same. A copy of one of my father's letters follows these pages.

The text of my father's letter sounded nearly normal to me. Of course, if it had included statements that would have suggested anything but normalcy, the letter would not have passed the censors. But my parents, soon after the government take-over by the Nazis, had agreed on certain body motions and on particular words that had secret meanings to them and to them alone. I knew that his letters contained information that I did not understand. I also knew that I should not ask. To me, the letters merely meant that my father was still alive, somewhere, in a place that I had never seen and would never see. To my mother, the letters meant much more.

She was traveling every day, trying to make contacts and trying to find ways to have my father released. After several attempts, she was able to speak with the county leader of the Nazi party. He agreed to see her on September 10th. He told her that something might be done if the local head of the party in our suburb would write a favorable report about my father. Yes, he would immediately request such a report. That request was issued, but not for another twenty days.

Time passed. Days and weeks went by. Nothing happened. My mother was frustrated. On November 24th she again tried to see the county leader. She was told that he was out of town - even though another visitor to the office recognized his voice in the next room.

She returned to the county seat every day. On November 30th she was told that the report from the local party office had arrived. It would be forwarded to the state offices. They would have to decide. It finally arrived on the desk of a state party official on December 19th. Although we did not know it at the time, the report contained the sentence, "Mr. Streufert still has not learned to use the obligatory 'Heil Hitler' when he meets other people on the street."

In the meantime, my father's absence had become a way of life for me. I had not seen him for five months. Life continued. Air raids. Attempts to obtain food. Transfer to a far away school - all schools in the city had been severely damaged by bombs. The city of Kiel had become much too dangerous for children. All schools had been closed.

We lived the "normal" life of people in a war. Occasionally I would look at a picture of my father. It was a friendly picture, not the "formal" kind from the time he had been a Senator. In this one, he had his arms around my mother. He was smiling. I would look at him. And sometimes I would kiss the picture, but then I felt stupid. Why should I kiss a picture!? After all, it was only a picture!

Christmas. The first Christmas without my father. It was strange. There were no presents to speak of. There was no joy. My mother tried to make everything appear as normal as possible. But it was not. And the war still was not over.....

Konzentrationslager
Hamburg-Neuengamme

Neuengamme, 1.10.44

Der Tag der Entlassung kann jetzt noch nicht angegeben werden. Besuche im Lager sind verboten. Anfragen sind zwecklos.

Auszug aus der Lagerordnung:
Jeder Häftling darf im Monat 2 Briefe oder Postkarten empfangen und absenden. Eingehende Briefe dürfen nicht mehr als 4 Seiten à 15 Zeilen enthalten und müssen übersichtlich und gut lesbar sein. Geldsendungen sind nur durch Postanweisung zulässig, deren Abschnitt nur Vor-, Zuname, Geburtstag, Häftlingsnummer trägt, jedoch keinerlei Mitteilungen. Geld, Fotos und Bildereinlagen in Briefen sind verboten. Die Annahme von Postsendungen, die den gestellten Anforderungen nicht entsprechen, wird verweigert. Unübersichtliche, schlecht lesbare Briefe werden vernichtet. Im Lager kann alles gekauft werden. Nationalsozialistische Zeitungen sind zugelassen, müssen aber vom Häftling selbst im Konzentrationslager bestellt werden. Lebensmittelpakete dürfen zu jeder Zeit und in jeder Menge empfangen werden.

Der Lagerkommandant

Meine Liebe

Deine lieben Briefe habe ich von dir erhalten auch den vom 17.9. Ebenfalls sind zwei Pakete auf einmal angekommen. Vielen Dank meine Liebe. Vielleicht hast du mal wieder etwas zu schicken, dann bitte keine verderbliche Ware. Mache dir um mich keine unnötigen Sorgen. Ich will dies überstehen, im Bewusstsein meiner Unschuld. Behaltet mich weiter lieb, du und unsere [illegible]. Wir wollen und werden uns gesund wiedersehen. Was macht Heinz [illegible]. Gibt es Nachricht von ihm? Schickt bitte Briefmarken, Schnürsenkel und Stiefelfett mit. Mir geht es sonst gut.

Tausend Grüße und Küsse [illegible]
[illegible]

[illegible]

TO FORGIVE OR NOT TO FORGIVE....

Sometime, during the Autumn of 1944, a Lutheran minister said a few words during his Sunday sermon, words that clearly displeased the Nazis. They always monitored Sunday sermons. Whatever a minister or priest might say was reported to the party office. One Sunday, the minister of the local church included the sentence, "Thou shalt obey God more than men." That was too much.

The Nazis did not approve of religion. They had invented their own "religious" approach. They resurrected the old concept "predetermination." The rise of Hitler, the victory of the Nazi party and the future victory of German armies over all enemies were "predetermined" by fate. If party members wanted to be religious, they were to claim an orientation called "Gottgläubig," suggesting some kind of belief in the existence of a deity. What kind of a god it might be was left quite unclear. But the churches, in other words organized religion, were rejected and shunned by the Nazis. Organized religion was too dangerous for them. Any institution that they could not directly control might create dissent.

"Thou shalt obey God more than men" was taken as a challenge to Nazi authority. Hitler and his cohorts demanded complete subservience to the views and demands of the party. The reaction to the sermon was swift. During the night following the sermon, the minister disappeared. He spent two months in a concentration camp. He was released shortly before Christmas, likely with a strong admonition never to violate the written and unwritten rules of "National Socialism" again.

My mother contacted him. They communicated. I do not know whether they ever met; it would have been much too dangerous to meet in public. I know that they managed to send notes to each other through someone else. At one time, the minister wrote a lengthy letter to my mother. To protect him, she transcribed his words into a rare and outdated version of shorthand that very few people could read. She omitted his name and signature from the translation, just in case someone decided to have the text deciphered. The original note was

111

burned.

The first page of his letter read:

"I did not have the opportunity to write to you during the Christmas holidays, but I do not want this year end before I have at least finished a letter that will reach you."

"I can well understand what you have been through during these months - and what you will go through in the months to come. No human being can take that burden off your shoulders. Those who could help are persuaded that their actions are legitimate and right, permissible by a higher cause. I am sure you will not understand them, especially their belief that their actions are just and right. I understand their views but I do not share them. That is how they are."

"It reminds me of the New Testament. The Romans, who arrested and crucified Christ, were absolutely sure that they were doing the right thing for their country. They saw Jesus as an enemy of their state and their country. It would not be fair to view the Romans as nasty and 'bad' people. They merely did not know and did not understand the will of God, and, consequently, they accumulated a guilt that cannot be forgiven. But, we are not their judges: Only God can judge them."

"That is also true today. No matter how much we may be tempted to become bitter, to accuse those people of inhumanity, it is not useful to succumb to such feelings. It distracts us from the only thing that is necessary, the one thing we should do. We should fully and completely accept God's will. Jesus, as he suffered, was not concerned with the lack of humanity of his torturers. He focused upon God's sacred and inexplicable will - and he obeyed even as he died. His last words were not an accusation of his enemies, rather he was asking that they be forgiven. And only through this absolute obedience to God did he accomplish something that no other human has ever accomplished: He transformed the nastiness of his enemies into God's blessings. He changed death into life."

"I don't know whether you can understand all this, Mrs. Streufert. There are things, and they are the most important things in our lives, that cannot be understood by our rational minds. There are insights that we can only gain through suffering. One of these insights is the complete acceptance of what happens, the complete acceptance of God's will....."

My mother and I talked a bit about this letter. Complete acceptance? Total forgiveness of what the Nazis were doing to my father and to so many other people? Yes, I could comprehend how their basic tenets of thought would lead to their actions. But those tenets themselves were inhumane and basically flawed! To me, "ends could never justify the means" when those means were obviously and completely "immoral." Was religion not somehow about morality? Most of all, why would God allow a few monsters to torture and, as it later turned out, kill more than eleven million people? Was this the same God that demanded that we should "love thy neighbor" and command "thou shalt not kill"?

I could not understand such a God. And I could not simply accept and forgive Nazi actions.

LIFE IN THE CONCENTRATION CAMP

We were allowed to send food packages of a specified size
to my father. It was difficult to gather enough food to fill even
a small package; there was little to eat at this time. Because of
my father's absence, the food rations assigned to our family had
been further reduced. We mailed whatever we could obtain.
Food was generally permitted by concentration camp rules, with
some exceptions. For example, a loaf of bread was not accepted
because it could conceal a weapon. Without food packages from
relatives, the prisoners would soon starve to death. They were
fed no more than a thin vegetable soup once a day. That was all.
The statement on the letterhead of the camp, suggesting that
"anything" at all was available for purchase inside the camp was,
of course, gross nonsense.

We were allowed to include cigarettes as part of the food
packages. In the concentration camp those cigarettes could be a
life saver. Cigarettes became currency among the inmates.
Cigarettes could purchase food. Those who were completely
dependent on nicotine would trade their food packages for
cigarettes.

We found out about life in the camp from another
inmate. During January 1945, a very thin and ill-looking man
knocked on our door. He had been in the concentration camp
Neuengamme with my father. Arrested on the same day, he had
initially been interred at Dragon Lake as well. Both men were
transferred to Neuengamme. During the Weimar Republic, our
visitor had been a member of the State Parliament in Kiel. Since
he had not been nationally prominent and since a review of his
actions during the Nazi period had turned up nothing unfavorable, he was released in mid-December. Initially, he had been too
sick to travel. Once he regained some stamina, he came to see
us.

He started to talk about life in the camp. His tales were
so horrible that I left the room soon after he had begun. The
tales made me feel sick, and sad, and angry - all at the same time.
I forced myself to go back to our living room about an hour later.
He was just telling my mother that the inmates were required to

114

stand in a long line every morning to be counted. They stood nude for the count. Even in the cold of winter! If someone was missing, was either too sick to show up or, most often, had died, all of the inmates had to stand and wait until that person was found. This torture exercise was called the "parade." Many among the inmates collapsed during these parades.

But he also told us how the inmates had tried to make life bearable and somehow interesting. They all knew that the Nazi regime could not last much longer. They spoke more freely with each other than would have been possible outside of the concentration camp. There were few spies among them - Nazi spies would not expose themselves to this torture and starvation.

Those who spoke foreign languages taught the others. My father, for example, who spoke German and English, decided to learn French. At other times, certain inmates discussed the future of Germany, how they would help to rebuild the government once the Nazi horror was over. They hoped to survive. My father hoped to survive. Later we found out that very few among those inmates actually did.

LETTERS AND PACKAGES

My father's last letter from Neuengamme arrived in mid-December. There was no letter in January. Packages we sent were returned. No reason was given. The same in February. One of the returned February packages was marked with a design that could have been a swastika, except that the lines at the ends of the cross were drawn through in both directions. My mother suspected the worst, but persisted in her hope. She asked several experts about the meaning of the design.

"It looks like a Kukenkreuz," she was told. Such a design was once used by an Austrian movement that had been quite similar to the Nazis.

She contacted the Nazi party at the county and at the state level. Nobody would speak with her. Letters addressed to the commander of the concentration camp were returned unopened. February and March passed. Still nothing. More packages kept coming back. Letters to my father were returned.

In April, we received a package. The return address was "The Commander of the Concentration Camp Hamburg-Neuengamme." My mother opened it. She found my father's clothes, the suit and underwear he had worn on the day he had been arrested. And there was a letter:

Concentration Camp
Hamburg-Neuengamme
 The Commander

 Enclosed you will find the clothing of August Streufert who died on 27 December 1944 of pneumonia.

Heil Hitler!

My mother collapsed. I did not know whether I should cry or try to comfort her. I did both. I touched her. Her heart was beating incredibly fast. I could feel it all over her body. It frightened me. I ran across the street to get our neighbors. I was sure that she would die. The neighbors sent me away. I walked across the meadows in back of our house. The grass was still there and the trees. Spring flowers were in bloom. But all that meant nothing. The world seemed so empty. The sun was shining, but it was grey. It was spring, but it could as well have been winter. Would life go on? Was it worth continuing? Why? Why?

A few weeks later we received another package. It was an urn with ashes. Whose ashes? According to the attached brief note, the urn contained the remains of my father. But, after all this time, how could it be? I wondered how many bodies had contributed to the dust in that urn. But, whatever it might be, we had something that we could bury, something that represented my father, even if only in spirit. It was the dust of all those people who suffered with him.

Very few of our neighbors came to the burial. They were too afraid to come. The Jansens came. The farmer next door. My best friend's family. And a few others. Most of the neighbors, in contrast, secretly shook my mother's hand - some time, somewhere, in some dark corner. We had joined the world of outcasts. It was dangerous to be seen talking with us, now that it was known my father had been arrested and killed by the Nazis. They did not know how or where he had died. Most did not know about concentration camps. We were not allowed to mentioned that word. But people in town did know that he had been killed as an "enemy of the Nazi state." That was enough.

THE LAST NAZI DAYS

INJURIES

It was April, 1945.   The local train from Kiel to Lübeck arrived late.   Trains no longer ran on schedule.   Even after the many passengers who lived in our suburb had gotten off, the train was still packed.   Travelers stood tightly squeezed against each other, even though this train was very long.

The signal turned green.   The engineer went to work. Rhythmic puffs of smoke climbed into the air.   At first, the six powered wheels of the old Prussian steam engine were spinning. Then the engineer released sand stored in a dome above the train engine's boiler.   It poured onto the rails and provided traction. The train began to move, to accelerate.   It would not go fast, certainly it would not try to attain maximum speed.   After all, the track would soon curve to the left and, in addition, the next station was only three miles away.   However, this train would never reach the next station.

During the last month of the war, the sky above us was owned by Allied aircraft.   German fighters, the few that were left, had been sent elsewhere.   Maybe they were used at the front lines, or maybe they were needed near Berlin.   Except for the very occasional use of anti-aircraft guns, there were few attempts to defend the air space around the city.   The lack of defense probably made sense: Kiel had turned into rubble.   Here and there, the walls of some building were still hinting at what was once a proud Hanseatic city.   But most of those buildings were burned out, all of them were without windows. Only the city hall tower was still standing.   Its old walls were too thick to be destroyed by bombs: It was pockmarked, but it stood.   Why defend a large sprawling pile of rubble?

Most of the anti-aircraft guns were also silent. British and American planes were flying barely above the tree tops. Anti-aircraft shells could not reach them.   The low altitude of the attacking planes provided advantages for the attackers.   They could hit their targets with greater precision. They could destroy any anti-aircraft positions that dared to respond to their presence. All in all, it was probably wiser not to challenge the planes.

Another thing had changed.   Once upon a time, the

Allied planes would fly in formations. Now they came one aircraft at a time, widely distributed. Nobody knew when a plane would show up or where it would fly next. Sirens that had reliably warned us of air attacks were wailing much too often. We had learned to ignore them.

Frequently, some Allied plane would show up without any warning at all. That is how it was at the moment when the local passenger train began to pull out of our railroad station.

The pilot must have seen the smoke of the steam locomotive as it started to accelerate. He must have seen the train move. He attacked.

My mother and I were sitting in the kitchen. Suddenly loud detonations rattled the windows. Pots and pans fell off a shelf. We could hear the loud humming of an aircraft engine. It was very close! We ran toward the basement, but the humming disappeared quickly. No more explosions. Carefully, we looked out of the front door. On the train track, quite close to our house, stood the train. The engine had been badly damaged. Steam and smoke emerged from strange places. That locomotive would no longer move.

But then we saw something else. It was horrible! People were climbing out of the passenger cars. Many had been hit by bomb fragments. Some ran, some walked, some limped, others were being carried. Those who were able to leave the train tried to get to nearby houses. About forty or fifty of them came toward us.

During the past few months, I had seen quite a few dead people - both women and children and even a few old men. But dead people lay still. They could not scream! These people were bleeding. They screamed. They cried for help.

I turned away. Despite all the destruction, all the death, all the horror that had become an everyday experience, this was more than I could stand.

But my mother would not let me turn away. "Go get our bandages!" she ordered. "Bring rubbing alcohol and any first aid creams you can find!" She was already busy gently removing the torn and bloody blouse of a woman. I brought whatever I could find: Hansa-Plast (like band-aids), bandages, medications that might help. All of it was soon used up.

"In the cabinet, in the hall, on the upper shelf, there is a white sheet. Get that!"

I found the sheet. My mother tore it into long strips. More people were bandaged. The terrazzo floor in our kitchen had turned red with blood.

I had not known that my mother knew something about treating injured people. She was not a physician or a nurse! Well, maybe she did not know much about what she was doing - maybe it was just necessary to keep the blood from flowing. I did not know. And it did not make any difference. By now I had gotten used to all the wounds, all that blood, and all the crying. I tried to help.

"Yes, it needs to be tight, but not too tight!" my mother instructed me as I was bandaging a child's arm. The blood still has to get through to her hand!" A lady who had not been hurt was helping take care of the injured. She smiled at me as though she was saying, "Good job!"

I continued to do what I could. A few more people came into the house. They were even worse off. And the sheet had been used up.

"Bring the table cloth from the living room!" I turned to go. But.... that was the table cloth I loved so much, the white on white one, with all those beautiful pictures, the pictures that were visible only if one looked carefully! I had always loved it! Often we had used it on special occasions, like Christmas. I hesitated.

"**That** table cloth?" I asked. For an instant, my mother stopped wrapping that last strip of sheet around the leg of an older man. She looked at me, very seriously. Then she smiled, just a bit.

"Yes, that tablecloth. Some things are more important."

SAVED BY A TREE

As I so often did, I was riding my bicycle. There was nothing else to do. All schools had been closed. The allied armies were only miles away. We could hear distant sounds of artillery.

Bombs were no longer falling. The larger planes carrying bombs had been replaced by low flying American planes that shot at anything moving. They were firing their machine guns, again and again. Trains, trucks and cars became frequent targets. A few milk cows and horses on nearby meadows were machine gunned. The death of these animals was somehow welcome. It meant less milk but a bit more meat. After all, that meat would be distributed among the residents of our suburb. Transportation to other places, except for military purposes, no longer existed.

I was riding my bike near our suburban train station when I saw one of those low altitude fighter planes. Its markings were American. I watched it carefully. As long as it did not head directly for me, I would be all right. They always fired their guns forward. If he headed my way, I could hide behind a bush or a tree so he would not see me. Or I could run into the nearest house that was still standing. People left their doors open: we all had to protect each other. But that plane headed east, then turned north along the highway that led toward the shore. There was no immediate danger.

While I was watching the plane, I did not pay attention to the road. The front wheel of my bike caught against the curb. I could no longer steer. I lost control and fell. As I hit the ground, one of my fingers was smashed between the metal of the bike and the stones that paved the street. It hurt. Something about my hand suddenly was not quite right. It started to swell. I rode home to let my mother inspect the damage.

"You better go to the physician," she decided. "That thumb looks like it may be broken. Let's let Dr. Peters have a look at it." During this time in the war, Dr. Peters, the nearest medical doctor, lived four miles away in the next town. All closer physicians had been drafted.

A couple of years ago, I would have had several choices

123

about how to get to Preetz, the town where Dr. Peters' had his office. But the trains did not run anymore, tracks were damaged in several places. Without available rails, the tracks could no longer be repaired. It was not worth repairing the railroads anyway; if any trains would have run, they would have been attacked by the fighter planes.

Buses had stopped running too. Gasoline and diesel fuel were distributed only to the military. The only way to get to Dr. Peters' office was to walk or to ride my bike. Well, I could still ride my bicycle, even if I could only use one hand.

Fortunately, most of the road to Preetz led through the "Bird Song" forest. The trees were very high beeches. Their widely spread crowns would hide me from any fighter planes. But after about two miles of forest I reached a stretch of open fields, about three-quarters of a mile long. Beyond that, the forest began again. For the moment I would be visible to the planes. Maybe a row of very old large oaks on both sides of the pavement, growing about sixty to seventy feet apart from each other, would help hide me from any planes in the sky....

I had already passed through the first part of the forest on my way to the physician. I was steering my bike with one hand. The hand with the damaged thumb was hurting. I let it hang straight down.

Suddenly I heard the humming of an airplane engine. It was obviously an allied plane: it sounded less rough than German aircraft. I looked up. There it was: a single propeller fighter, flying across the field on my right, probably the same plane I had seen earlier, or, at least, one that looked the same. It turned towards me. I dropped the bicycle and ran toward one of the large oaks. I had not quite reached the protection of that tree when I heard bullets whistling past me.

I stood behind the tree. I was breathing hard. But I felt less scared. From my hiding place I could not see the plane, yet its bullets would not hit me! They might hit the tree, but they would never get through that large oak, that much I knew. My heart was still pounding. I heard the plane fly over me, just above the tree top. Safe!

I stood still for another minute trying to catch my breath.

As I was about to check whether my bike was still okay, I noticed that the plane began to make a wide circle, turning around. He was coming back!

I quickly ran around the tree trunk to stand on the other side of the oak. I peeked around to see what the plane was doing. Was he going to shoot at me again? Why was he coming back? Would he even be able to see me? After all, there was another big tree on the opposite side of the pavement; would the branches of that oak not hide me? Probably not. After all, I had been able to see the plane turn around! He was coming! Only my face was showing. Could he see it? I moved around a bit more to stand behind the trunk at the opposite side from his approach. Again he fired his machine gun. This time he had aimed better: he knew where I was! Two bullets hit the opposite side of my tree, exactly where I had been standing a minute ago! Others whistled past.

Finally, it was over! The plane turned one more time, but not towards me. He was now flying west along the road toward the suburb where I lived.

I looked at the other side of the tree. Two bullets had made quite substantial holes - nobody could survive if they were hit by such bullets! I found my bicycle; it had not been hit. An hour or so later, Dr. Peters put a splint on my finger. Yes, it had been broken.

On my way back home, I carefully watched for planes. It was quiet. No more humming. No machine gun fire. I had time to think. How had I felt during that experience? What should I tell my mother and my friends? Somehow the experience had been strange; it had been so different from anything I had experienced before.

Sure, when that plane started to fire its machine gun at me, I had been afraid. My heart had pounded. But had my heart been beating wildly because I was afraid or because I was running so fast? When that plane came back, when he fired at me for the second time, at the instant when his aim had been much better, I had no longer been terribly scared. It had felt strange, weirdly uncomfortable. But it had also been funny, in a way that I would never be able to explain to anyone. It was

125

nearly like a weird game of hide-and-seek.

I compared this experience to the many air attacks of the past. I thought of the many days and nights we hid in the basement, waiting for the bombs to hit. That had been quite different! If one sits in the basement below the house, there is nothing one can do but wait. Bombs drop, one after another, coming closer and closer. The howling and whistling gets louder and briefer. Detonations, louder detonations, yet louder detonations! Each time the ground and the basement of the house trembles and shakes more and more.

As the detonations come closer and closer, we know the exact moment when we will either be alive or dead. We wait. Seconds turn into forever..... Then it finally happens: that incredibly loud noise, everything shakes, bricks, paint, anything loose flies around. But we are all still alive! Until the next time..... Or, in that very same instant, we could die. Whatever happened, happened. There was nothing one could do to save one's own life, or, for that matter, the lives of others. It happened, one either lived or one died. Over and over and over again.

But somehow this had been different. If you can hide behind a tree, if you can do something to try to protect yourself, that changes things! There had been something I could do! Actively! Yes, it had been scary, at least in the beginning. But, after I was able to hide behind the tree, I was no longer a "toy owned by chance." I was not entirely helpless.

Surely, it had not been a pleasant experience to be shot at by an airplane. But that terrible fear, that trembling horror, it had not been there.

When I came home, I was told that a plane had shot off the arm of a little girl I knew. Probably it was the same plane. The little girl was only three years old, too young to know she should hide from airplanes.

Postscript

Years later, I spoke about this experience with both German and American air force pilots that had flown low altitude attack missions during that war. I asked them the same question, again and again: "Why did you shoot at little children?" The answers were almost always the same.

"War is war."

The person operating the machine gun does not care very much, does not pay conscious moral attention to the "objects" in his sights. If that object - whatever it might be - moves, it is a target. It might be a train, a woman, a tank, a cow, a car, a horse, a truck or a child. It moves! And it moves within enemy territory! Start firing!

When questioned further, both German and the American pilots often admitted that they felt quite dissatisfied with their own actions during the war. But they generally did not feel guilty. Yes, possibly they had done things they were not proud of. But, it had been during the war. And: "War is war!"

A PISTOL

These were the very last days. No more food in the stores. Ration stamps were useless. No transportation. Occasional electricity. Only the water was still running. Thundering sounds of the battle were coming closer. We did not know whether we were hearing Russian guns to our east or American and British guns to our south. Clearly, the war was near its end. People started to behave strangely. They were afraid. All of us had become quite familiar with bombs. We knew what to expect during air attacks. We had been afraid, but somehow we understood that kind of war. None of us understood close artillery. We did not know what soldiers would do in battle. None of us knew what to expect, what would happen during the coming battle on the ground.

Indeed all of us were scared of the coming battle. Many were afraid of what the Nazis would now do. Hitler had demanded that every town should be defended to the last man - and "man" now included 12 year old children.

Even the local Nazis were getting desperate. They started to burn all of their files. For several days, fires were burning in back of the local administration building.

Factories and offices remained closed. Russian and Polish POWs who had been working for the farmers would no longer cooperate. There were whispered stories that some of the POWs had raped and killed young girls. And in even quieter whispers, people mentioned that the Nazis were killing their German neighbors. There were hints that they would murder all of those that they had never liked. Was it true? Were the Nazis afraid that, once Hitler's regime collapsed, those neighbors would accuse them of criminal acts? Were they trying to eliminate any witnesses that could testify against them? Were they afraid of future court cases that might be initiated by the victorious allies?

The worst fear for many of the local people was that Russian troops might arrive before the Americans or British could reach us. Nobody trusted Russian soldiers. Refugees who had been able to escape the eastern parts of Germany after the Russian troops occupied the area were telling horror stories.

They reported the rape of small children and of very old women. A Russian proverb supposedly promised a very long life to any man who would sleep with an extremely old woman. One lady from the East spoke of being raped by five Russian soldiers while her husband was held at gunpoint. When a Russian officer stormed in, he shot four of those soldiers and ordered the fifth to control the lady's husband. Then the officer raped the woman. Before he left, he shot and killed the fifth soldier.

But we heard funny stories as well. Many Russian soldiers were amazed about plumbing and electricity: "Water out of wall? Light out of ceiling?" Other Russians used insulators on telephone and power lines for target practice. They confiscated the watch of any German they saw. In the end they wore several watches on both of their arms and, in some cases, even on their legs!

The most frightening tales reported random killings of German civilians by Russians. In one case, it was said, about a hundred refugees were lined up on the side of a country road. Russian soldiers went down the line of women, children and a few old men who had been too old to be drafted into the German Army. One by one, the Russians killed each of their victims with a shot in the back of the neck. We met one refugee who was to be the next victim in that long line. Fortunately for him, the Russian soldiers stopped the mass murder to take cover when one of the few remaining German fighter planes was strafing their vehicles.

Supposedly one German civilian had greeted the arriving Russians with open arms. He told a Russian officer that he had always been a communist. He was delighted, he said, that the Russians had finally arrived. The Russian responded, "If you are a communist, you should have fought the Nazis!" He took out his pistol and shot the man in the face.

These were scary stories. How many of them were true? We did not know. But those reports of horrible occurrences certainly increased our fear of what might be happening to us, maybe tomorrow, maybe the next day, but certainly not before long.

A few weeks earlier, a woman from East Prussia stayed

with us. Her husband was a soldier assigned to the nearby anti-aircraft battery. She had left her two children with their grand-parents while she spent a little time with her husband on leave. As she tried to return home to her children and parents in East Prussia, she was stopped. The Russian army had advanced much further than Nazi radio admitted. East Prussia was already under Russian control. She was forced to turn back and once again stayed with us. She was desperate. She hoped and prayed that she would somehow find her family. But they had vanished, never to be seen again.

Now the front lines of the war were approaching us. The woman's husband told us that the nearby anti-aircraft battery had been mostly abandoned. Soldiers were discarding their uniforms and were putting on civilian clothes. Many were hiding. He brought us a few items that were no longer needed by the military. I received several small model airplanes - German, English and American. The models had been used to train soldiers on how to identify the shape of friendly and hostile aircraft.

He handed my mother a pistol and ammunition. "So you can protect yourself, if need be!" From the Russians? From the Nazis? From both?

She did not know how to use the weapon, but he was an excellent teacher. Of course, she would not be able to practice firing the gun - possession of a weapon was not permitted - and for the moment the Nazis were still in control. But the knowl-edge that she could protect us, if necessary, made her feel a bit more comfortable.

Several times during those last few nights of Nazi rule, we heard shots outside. Then her pistol was immediately at hand. Was it the war? Had the front lines reached us? Probably not. The sound of artillery in the distance had become louder, but it was not yet here. No, these were Nazis shooting. Several neighbors were killed during that time. Fortunately, nobody decided to threaten my mother or me. That pistol was not needed after all.

A few days later, it was over. The mayor of Kiel had contacted the Allied forces. The city would not resist occupation by British or American soldiers.

About noon the next day, an open jeep with a large white star drove into town. It was not a red star! These were Americans, not Russians! Two men in a uniform that looked quite different from those we had seen for so many years got out of the jeep at the railroad crossing and looked around. They appeared entirely unafraid! One of them laughed. They talked to each other, got back into the jeep and continued on.

It was incredible! This was the battle we had feared so much? One jeep with occupants who just looked around? And laughed? Nothing more?

A few hours later, a couple of tanks with the same white stars rattled down the street. As a last "defense," the Nazis had dug up the road a few hundred feet from us. They had planted "I" beams deeply into the ground. The metal barriers pointed into the sky at about a 45 degree angle, facing in both directions. After all, who knew from which direction the "enemy" would come.

As the tanks reached the barrier, the first in line stopped. A crew member got out and tapped his finger against the beams. He smiled, climbed back into the tank. The engine howled as the metal monster continued forward. The beams just crumpled.

For us, the war was over, even though we could still hear guns in the distance. It must have been Russian artillery.

A few days later, the newly established "military government" ordered us to turn in all our weapons at a central collection point. My mother gave up her pistol. Nobody questioned whether it had been legally owned. Our pistol was thrown into a cardboard box with so many others. A number of full cardboard boxes were sitting on the ground. It was surprising to see how many guns the people of our town had owned.....

131

MRS. KIPSIND

As the Russian troops came closer and closer, the stream of refugees from the East increased. Refugees who had left earlier were able to get onto overcrowded trains for at least part of the way. They were the first to arrive. Those who left only a few days before the Russians armies conquered their farms, villages and cities crowded onto worn out trucks, rode by the dozens on small horse drawn wagons, pedaled their bicycles or, in most cases, walked - nearly always carrying their most important belongings in one or two small bags.

Those who left at the last minute frequently did not survive. They were caught in front line military traffic, were ordered off the roads by soldiers and in many cases were killed during some battle. Many were seriously wounded or died when Russian airplanes strafed the columns of refugees heading west. No medical services were available to the injured. Some casualties were caused by the refugees themselves. Fights erupted when more people than feasible tried desperately to get onto that last bus or that last horse-drawn wagon heading west.

Now they moved past our house, still westward, away from the Russians. They were tired and hungry. This time the flow of refugees was heading toward the bombed out city, just as it had moved east, away from that city, during the days and nights of many air attacks. These refugees streamed past us by the thousands. They passed our house during the last few days of Nazi rule. They continued to come after the western allies had already occupied the area where we lived. The stream of people seemed endless.

Some time ago, we had decided not to join them. We had been hoping that the British or the American troops would get to us before the Russians would. Once we had seen the white star on that jeep, we felt safe. Now the Russians would not come. We definitely could stay. Many of the refugees from the east decided to stay in our town as well. They needed a roof over their heads and a bed to sleep in. Such amenities, however, were not easy to find.

Refugees who were too tired, too worn, too starved to

continue, were placed into local homes. Rooms were rationed. Every local couple was permitted to keep one room of their house or apartment. One additional room was assigned to groups of male or female children over the age of twelve. Kids under twelve of either gender had to sleep together, often in the same bed. Kitchens and bathrooms were to be shared with refugee families. Living rooms were turned into bedrooms.

Our house quickly filled.

One evening, Mrs. Kipsind knocked on our door. She had walked, so she told us, all the way from Masuren, about 500 miles. It seemed an unlikely feat, yet - despite her 84 years - she seemed quite physically able. Maybe her story was true....

She informed us in her half-Polish, half-German words that she was very tired. She needed to sleep. She wanted to stay just that one night. Tomorrow she would definitely continue west.

I found it very difficult to understand her. Her few German words were spoken in a broad East Prussian accent. To us kids, the East Prussians sounded as though they were speaking "with a hot potato in their mouth." But somehow my mother understood what the old lady wanted.

"We have no more beds. All our rooms are filled with refugees, but if you want to sleep in the hallway, on a lawn chair, that will be fine."

We got the chair from our garden. We found yet another blanket. Mrs. Kipsind was immediately asleep. The next morning she announced that she had changed her mind. She would stay.

"But Mrs. Kipsind, we don't have a bed for you. And everyone has to walk through the hallway - it will be difficult for you to get any sleep!"

"That doesn't make any difference," she said in her strange accent. "I am not continuing on. Not one more yard. I am living here."

There were no more rooms in our suburb. Too many homes had been destroyed by bombs. Too many refugees had decided to stay. We had no choice. She had to sleep in our hallway.

In the evening she would fall asleep early, making it clear to everyone that she did not want to be disturbed. If anyone talked in an adjacent room or if someone walked less than carefully through the hall, she would resent it. Her anger was extremely problematic. After all, she possessed a very special weapon.

Next to Mrs. Kipsind's chair stood a glass jar. A few very small holes were punched through its lid. If anyone bothered the old lady, if anyone spoke loudly when she tried to sleep, she would unscrew the top of the jar and, with incredible speed for her 84 years, would race toward that person to dump the jar's contents on that individual. The jar contained body lice that she carefully collected from her skin and her clothing. She made sure that she did not injure the insects as she placed them into her jar. To make sure that nobody would deprive her of her weapon, Mrs. Kipsind always carried the jar with her.

Most of us took great care not to annoy the old lady. After all, we could not get rid of her or her lice. Personal insecticides, just like everything else those days, were not available. Even if we had been able to obtain some substance that might have killed her lice, she would have refused to use it. After all, she would have lost her most effective weapon. She knew the source of her power. What can an 84-year-old woman do to get her own way, unless she has some means to control other people?

Even lice have their uses.

THE FORESTER

"The forester is dead," they whispered.

I had always liked him. Mr. Hartmann had been a friendly man. He had loved the forest and its animals. I well remembered the baby deer he raised in his garden; somehow a doe had died soon after its fawn was born. The forester would not let the little creature die too. The Hartmann family raised the fawn, first nursing it with a baby bottle and later feeding it cabbage and other vegetables that they grew in their garden. It was something they wanted to do despite the lack of food during the war. Their little deer baby was important. It had become family, and food was shared among family members.

The forester had two children - a son, about four years older than I, and a daughter. She was in my grade at school and we knew each other well. I had often visited her and her family in the forest. One might say I was as much "in love" with her as an eight to ten year old boy can be with a girl of the same age. Other kids in our school knew it; they often teased me.

"Siegfried has a girl friend!!!" they would sing out in that sequence of tones that kids use all over the world use to torture their age mates. Apparently, spending time with a girl was unacceptable for someone my age! But it certainly was not unacceptable to me. Their taunting was not meant to be friendly, yet it did not bother me.

"Are you jealous?" I often asked. They would look strangely at me; I guess they were unable to make sense of my response

Now her father, Mr. Hartmann, was dead. He had died during the night after the Allied forces had first been seen in Kiel and in our suburb. When I heard about her father's death, I wanted to go see my "girlfriend" to comfort her. But my mother would not let me go. It was still too dangerous to walk around outside.

"Why did he die?" I asked. "Was he sick?" I could hardly believe that he might have been deathly ill. I had recently seen him walk past our house, it seemed to me that it had been just yesterday!

135

I was shocked when I heard how he died, yet it was not hard to believe what had happened. The forester had been shot. Yes, it was true; yesterday he had come into town. He tried to find some food for his family. But he had not been able to obtain anything. While walking from store to store, hoping that one of them might be open, he happened to meet some of the local Nazi leaders on the street. They appeared to be quite nervous. After all, the Allies would be here soon. One jeep, the one with the white star, had already driven through town.

"Good day," the Forester had said to the Nazis. He did not greet them with the required "Heil Hitler." And then he had added, "I guess your time is up, isn't it?" Supposedly, he had laughed a bit, too. Mr. Hartmann was obviously glad that the Nazi horror would soon be over. He had never liked Hitler and his followers.

That night, about eleven o'clock, someone knocked on the door of the forester's house. It was pitch dark. Mr. Hartmann turned on the light and walked toward the door. Who could it be? Then, as he glanced through a window near his front door, he saw Nazi uniforms. The men outside had pistols in their hands.

He turned and ran toward the phone on the wall. Thank God, it was still working! He dialed the emergency number. Someone answered. He reported an armed robbery.

But he could not finish his telephone call. The light inside was on. They could see him through the window. Shots rang out. The forester collapsed.

Nobody was sure how many bullets hit him. But he had already reported his address before he fell. About three hours later, an emergency vehicle arrived, already manned by Allied soldiers. They came too late. The forester was dead.

OCCUPATION

DISBELIEF

It had been three or four days since the Allies took control. The government offices in our town were open again. We were told that we were under British occupation. The English officer in charge of our district had selected one of the townspeople to work with the British military government. It was someone who had not been tainted by Nazi activity. He was to be the German representative of Allied forces for the town. As his first official action, the new quasi-mayor cut the swastika out of the official seal of his office.

A British truck or tank would occasionally move through town. The Allies seemed to be in control. It seemed safe to go outside again. The Nazis were not leaving their homes. Probably they were afraid. I asked my mother whether she thought it would be all right to visit one of my friends. "I think so," she said. "But be careful. Just in case."

There was nothing to be afraid of. In a way, everything looked as it had before - except the Nazi flag was no longer flying in front of the local administration building. There still was no food in any of the stores. There was still rubble where houses once stood, just as it had been a week earlier when the Nazis were still running the town. But there were no brown shirts to be seen. Not even one. Not anything with even a litle bit of brown coloring.

I went to my best friend's house. He was not home. I decided to visit another boy with whom I had occasionally played in the past. He, his parents and some other people I did not know sat and talked in their living room. It seemed to be a rather lively debate.

As I arrived, the mother of my playmate was just saying, "But I can't believe it! The British are lying! Germans would not do anything like that!"

Her husband agreed. "No, I don't believe it either. This is a country with culture, with ethics. Ours is the country that has brought forth poets and writers and famous musicians. It cannot happen here. We are not barbarians."

I wondered what they were talking about.

Someone else, a man whom I had not met before, broke in, "I am not so sure. Those Nazis were just lower class bums. I think they were capable of killing people. Not millions of people. Probably not even thousands. No sane person would do anything like that. But a few - I could believe that."

"Besides," added my classmate's mother, "they needed workers and soldiers. They wouldn't have killed the very people they needed! Why would they bring all those Poles and Russians to work in the shipyards? Most of them could not even understand instructions on what to do. I was working there in one of the offices. I know. And, of course, the POWs did not want to build our ships anyway. Actually I don't blame them. No, the Nazi government would not have killed people who speak German and could have worked in the factories! It does not make sense!"

What were they talking about? About people that the Nazis had killed?

My friend's father seemed to have the same opinion as his wife. "Well, we all know that they punished people who publicly disagreed with them. But that news item about concentration camps, I can't believe that. That is obviously Allied propaganda. They want us to forget about the Nazi past. They want us to think the Nazis were bad people. Well, some of them probably were. But most of them were not criminals. There were no concentration camps!"

"Excuse me," I said. Everyone looked at me.

"My father was killed in a concentration camp." I spoke quietly but firmly. They all looked shocked. They had no idea how to respond. It was an uncomfortable silence.

"I have to go home now," I added.

"I WILL BE BACK...."

During the war, many Polish and Russian prisoners of war lived in our suburb. Several had been assigned to work for the local farmers; they lived in the same rooms where German farm laborers had lived before. Other POWs were assigned to rooms in nearby barracks. Most of them had been employed in the shipyards on the eastern side of the Kiel fjord, across the water from downtown Kiel. You could easily tell the POWs apart from anyone else - most continued to wear their old military uniforms, but signs of rank and decorations had been removed. On the back of their uniform jackets the letters K G were emblazoned in bright white writing, Kriegs-Gefangener (= War Captive, i.e., POW). Their contributions to the German wartime economy were sorely needed. German employees of the shipyards as well as German farm laborers up to age fifty had been drafted. During the last few months of the war, people even above fifty had to serve in auxiliary military positions.

Most prisoners of war were nice people. The Nazis had issued an official government rule stating that German citizens would not be permitted to talk to POWs, except to give them work instructions. But in our suburb, that rule was not taken very seriously. I often spoke with the Russians who were working for the farmer next door. Their German was broken, but good enough to communicate. My father had developed a good relationship with them. He gave them a number of things that they needed, once even a razor with blades. It was a bit danger-ous: POWs were not allowed to own anything that could be remotely conceived as a weapon. For that matter, all gifts to POWs were prohibited. But how would anyone know? After all, they were people, just like us. Neither they nor we had started this war....

After the war ended, the Russian prisoners were rapidly returned to their country. A few Poles remained for a longer period of time. Understandably, some among the prior prisoners of war were hostile toward the German population. Of course, the Allied victory provided them with rights and privileges that they had not had as prisoners. A few of them believed that the changed situation gave them rights and privileges of "victors," opportunities that they would no longer have after they returned to their own countries.

Nonetheless, there were many among the POWs who did not insist on special treatment. They had gotten along with the local population during the war, and they would get along with us now. After all, we were all people. We were all hungry. About this time we started having long conversations with a Polish intellectual. Prior to the war, he had held some position at the University of Warsaw. Now that the war was over, we were able to talk freely and extensively with him. His German was excellent. On many evenings, he and some grown-ups I knew would talk about politics, about philosophy, about art and music. There were even debates and tentative attempts to define our common European future. Economics and the differences between socialist and capitalist thinking played some role in those conversations. Sometimes I was allowed to listen. Occasionally I found those discussions boring. But sometimes they fascinated me.

I remember the man from Warsaw University well. But my memory is much more precise about another Polish man. I recall his features precisely! Yet I saw him only once for a very short time.

I was playing in back of our house. Anke, now a nineteen year old girl from next door, came running towards me as fast as she could. She looked scared. Her face was bright red. Her dress was ripped at the top. When she was only a few feet from me, she turned toward our back door and yanked it open. She knew that we never locked that door.

My mother was in the kitchen as Anke ran in, "He is after me!" she called out. "That Polish man!"

My mother closed the door behind her. "Quick, jump out of our bedroom window on the other side of the house. He won't see you!"

The man came running. He was not quite as fast as Anke. He looked around. "Where is she?" He stared at me, anger and something else that I could not identify in his eyes.

"Whom are you looking for?" I tried to cover for her. But it was scary. The man seemed ready to hit anyone in his way.

"She came here!" he yelled angrily. This was followed by something I could not understand in Polish. But it sounded ominous.

Then he saw the back door to our house. He jumped up the three steps and smashed the door wide open.

"Where is she?"

My mother was amazingly calm. "Where is who?" she asked gently.

"The woman! You are hiding her!" He pushed his way past my mother, running from room to room, encountering only the refugees who now lived all over our house. Then he came to our bedroom. It was empty. He saw the open window, ran towards it, then looked outside. Anke was nowhere to be seen.

Slowly, very slowly he walked back into the kitchen. There he stood for a minute or so, staring at my mother. His eyes were filled with anger.

"I will be back!" His voice was very hard and threatening.

With one more angry look at my mother, he left. He paid no attention to me.

From that day on, we always locked the back door to the house, even during the daytime.

But he never returned.

AN ENTRY INTO THE HUNGER COOKBOOK

Occasionally, I liked the dinners my mother managed to prepare. Of course, she had a very difficult time. Basic food staples were unavailable. Spices, except for one, had not been seen in the stores for years. Salt, well, sometimes we had some. We relied mostly on our own garden and on whatever we could find - or whatever the local farmers would give us if we pleaded long enough.

My mother made a wonderful bean soup with potatoes, carrots and other home grown vegetables from our garden. While my father was still alive, he had built cages for about forty rabbits. We raised them on grass and dandelions that we harvested next to a railroad track. The rabbits provided us with occasional meat. But a neighbor had to kill those poor animals - we were much too attached to them to do it ourselves. In return, the neighbor got to keep about every fifth rabbit.

At other times, my mother made cabbage soup. She cooked kale and other green things from the garden. I did not appreciate most of the "green dishes" very much. But when one is hungry, one eats every last bite of everything, even if it does not taste good.

To survive, we had learned to use the nearby forest as a source of food as well. For one hundred metric pounds of beech-nuts, we would receive one pound of margarine. It took hours to find this many nuts! At other times, we collected mushrooms and raspberries. My mother cooked rose hips and camomile flowers into a kind of jelly, without sugar of course.

A group of Italians who worked in the shipyards were combing the nearby forested hills for snails. They would boil them in metal containers that had once held tar for use in road construction. Of course, water in those containers would quickly turn black. The snails would also turn black. But that did not seem to bother those gentlemen. We called their favorite food "Escargot Noir."

The longer the war lasted, the more difficult it became to obtain enough food to eat at least one meal a day. By the end of the war, after the destruction of all means of transportation, it was even harder. Now we had to provide for the refugees as well. In addition to the eight hundred of us who had lived in our suburban town during the war, we now had an additional fifteen hundred refugee mouths to feed. As a result, we all literally faced starvation.

Fortunately, after a while, the Americans decided to help. A representative of the U.S. government met with a German official. He wanted to know what was needed most. There was no doubt in the German's mind. "Korn!" he said.

Korn, in the German language, means grain. The American, however, understood the English word "corn." Liberty ships were loaded with corn and sent to Germany. Suddenly we had bread again. But it was yellow. Yellow Bread? What is it? In Central Europe, corn had never been used for human consumption. If it was grown at all, it was fed to hogs or chickens. Not even cornstarch was known, only potato starch. People asked each other: "Is that really bread? What did they put in there? Is it safe to eat?"

Nonetheless, it was quite a relief to get **something** to put in our mouths. True, some people became ill after eating the yellow bread, probably because they were eating a physiologically unfamiliar food after starving for so long. Yet we learned to love it, or at least to eat it. It meant survival!

Until the corn arrived, we had to try to survive on our own. Some people did starve to death. We did not. How did we get enough food to keep us alive?

Our town was part suburb of the nearby city; in part, however, it was still a farming town. Of course, the farmers harvested foodstuffs. And, fortunately, it was summer. Again and again we asked the farmers for something to eat. Most of the time they would respond with a phrase that was and continues to be so typical for that part of Northern Germany: "Mal sehn...." ("We'll see..."). And nothing would happen. But we would not give up. We asked, again and again and again. After a while, the farmers would give in. We might receive a yellow beet or, if we were very lucky, even a white sugar beet. Normally, all those beets would have been fed to the pigs. But at the end of the war there were fewer pigs than before. The farmers were hungry just like the rest of us. Although the government attempted to count the number of animals any farmer owned, and although the authorities tried to assure that all animals would go to market, there were always ways to sidetrack an animal. The farmers liked to eat pork. That, in turn, reduced the pig population. As a consequence, a few beets would be left over. They could be given away.

If we were very, very, very lucky, the farmer next door would let us have a half pint of milk. What a cause for celebration!

But milk was a rare event indeed. Getting a beet was a bit more common. How do you cook a good meal with only one beet? It may be surprising how many possibilities exist! There certainly is not room for all those wonderful beet recipes in this book. Here are some recipe names that a "hunger cookbook" could hardly do without:

Raw Beets
Sliced Beets
Mashed Beet
Boiled Beets
Chopped Beets

Now for some of the special Sunday dinners:
Sliced Beets with Mashed Beets
Mashed Beets over Boiled Beets, served with Sliced Beets
Fried Beets

Well, I will make an exception. Considering how wonderful fried beets are, let me provide the complete recipe. I know the preparation procedure exactly, after all I watched my mother many times when she prepared this rare delicacy!

FRIED BEETS

Ingredients
One or, if possible, several beets,
A few grains of wheat,
Water,
Salt, if available.

Preparation
Determine which farmer is about to harvest wheat. Select one who has very bad equipment, that is a harvesting machine that is not able to capture each grain from the stalks. Walk slowly and carefully across the recently harvested field. Do not delay. A day later no grains of wheat will be left on the ground. Remember, you are not the only person who is scouring the ground for a few grains! If possible, make friends with the farmer beforehand. He may even allow you to walk directly behind his harvesting machine. You will find more.

Take your precious grains home. Start a fire with kindling wood (since gas and electricity are no longer available). Place a frying pan above that fire. The pan must be dry (you don't have any fat you could put into the pan anyway). Roast the wheat grains until they are brown. They may remind you of coffee beans (if you still remember what those things used to look like; real coffee beans, even bad ones, have not been available for years).

Now find your coffee mill. Yes, the old one you inherited from grandmother, the one with the handle that turns on top. It is probably in back of something else - it has not been used since the store sold out of coffee beans. Grind the browned grains of wheat. True, the powder looks nearly like ground coffee! Now you remember coffee, right?

Let yourself do what you most want to do. Make some coffee out of that powder. But stop! Don't drink it! It tastes awful anyway. Besides, we need it for our fried beets, remember?

Keep boiling that "coffee" until half of it has boiled away. Now you have a nicely steamed up kitchen, and it smells like something or other. The kitchen has not smelled like anything for months, true? Now that liquid you are boiling is beginning to look a bit funny. It has little "fatty" bubbles on it. This is the "fat" we will use to fry our beet(s).

Pour a lot of our "fatty" liquid into the frying pan. I am sure you washed the pan in the meantime. Without detergent, of course. We have not had any soap for at least a year.

If you like, peel the beet(s). But if you are very hungry, don't peel them. Throwing out the peels would be a terrible waste! Just wash the beet(s). Cut into slices. "Fry" the slices in the liquid until brown.

And now, the most fabulous dinner of the month is ready to be served! Bon Appetit! Or as we said in Germany: "Guten Apetit!"

But I am sure I don't have to wish you a healthy appetite. If you are starved, that appetite is never missing...no matter how awful your food tastes.

INVITATION TO THAI

Not long after the war ended, the British forces held a military maneuver in northern Germany. We had no idea whom they considered their potential enemy. The German armies had been beaten and the soldiers were disarmed. The destruction of German military equipment and fortifications was in progress. The submarine bunkers in Kiel were being blown up. Were the British worried about the Russians? We could not figure it out.

Someone in town reported that British soldiers had put up a very large number of tents in the nearby forest. Supposedly thousands of soldiers were hiding there, armed to the teeth. Someone wondered whether they had come to kill us after all?

My friend Friedrich-Karl and I were not in the least concerned. A fear that the British would attack a town they had already occupied was like believing in the Boogey Man. We had never believed in the boogey man - not even when we were little. So we decided to go to the forest. We wanted to see for ourselves.

Indeed, we found a lot of British soldiers. But as for the large numbers of troops someone had reported - that was not quite true. For a while, we watched one group of uniformed men from some distance. They were sitting around an open fire. A kettle, probably full of water, was hanging above the fire. Flames were leaping up, blackening the kettle. Considering the flames under the kettle, we thought it good that it had rained recently. There would be no forest fire.

Should we dare to approach them? Should we try to talk to those people? Would they see us as "enemies," even though we were just kids? After all, just a short time ago, Germany and England had been at war.

We decided to risk it and walked toward them. At that time, we had been taking English lessons for about four months. Surely we would know enough English to speak with the soldiers! It should work. At least, we would try.

As we approached, all of the soldiers in the group were looking at us. Two kids, they may have thought. What would those kids want?

"Hello, " we said cautiously. A few of the men started to smile. These two kids speak English! And after a few more words on our part, nearly all of them seemed enthusiastic. They all started talking to us at the same time. This was fun! But then one of them asked: "Would you like a coop of thai?"

Well there was no question in our minds about the man's first three words. They were offering us something or other. But, what in the world was a "coop of thai?" What did it matter? We would accept. After all, why not?

"Yes, please!"

More extensive conversation turned out to be a bit difficult. These soldiers did not come from England at all; they were from Scotland!

"That is somewhere north of England, is it not?" The answer to our question was hard to understand. The "yes" came through clearly, but it was then followed by a lengthy explanation. Together, the two of us made out about every third word. Something about a place north of another place called Edinburgh.

Admittedly, the communication problem was in good part a lack of knowledge on our part. Studying English three hours a week for four months doesn't yield a large vocabulary.

When the "thai" came, it was tea. Very strong. But not bad at all. And there was sugar in it. And milk. Wonderful! We stayed for another fifteen minutes or so before heading home.

People in town were eager to find out what was going on out there, deep in that forest. As we returned, we told them that those English soldiers were just great. Too bad that they had set up camp out there in the forest. They should have come to the middle of town instead. That way everyone could have met them.

Well, a little later we did have English soldiers in town. Then, however, it turned out not to be so wonderful.

CAP ARCONA

Only a few days after the war ended, we received news about the last days of the Concentration Camp Neuengamme. The radio stations were broadcasting again. News and commentary was edited by the Allied forces. Nazi atrocities were a frequent topic of those radio broadcasts. One offered a chronicle of events at the Camp Neuengamme.

We were told that inmates who were still alive as the allied forces approached were crowded into freight cars and taken to the Baltic Sea. The train arrived in a freight yard, somewhere near the port of Lübeck. Then everyone was herded onto the passenger ship Cap Arcona. The vessel had just brought refugees from the east. Now it was ordered to head out to sea again, destination unknown. The captain would receive instructions at a later time. Nazi SS soldiers in uniform were placed on board to ensure that the orders would be carried out. The SS raised the military flag and the ship headed out to sea.

A few hours later, still within sight of shore, the Cap Arcona was attacked by British aircraft. It was hit and sunk. Most concentration camp inmates were much too weak to swim ashore. Those who had still been strong enough were, in most cases, shot and killed by Nazi SS troops as they approached the beach. A few were saved by civilian fishing boats. Some of those boats returned to Holstein where British troops were now arriving. Others finally docked in the state of Mecklenburg. There Russians occupation forces had arrived.

One Neuengamme inmate, one of the few who had been saved by a fishing boat from Holstein, visited my mother a few weeks after the war was over. He had known my father well, so he said. He was adamant that my father did not die in the camp. My father had been on the ship Cap Arcona. And, this man assured us, it had been my father who negotiated with the captain of the ship. The two men had agreed that the crew and the inmates would surprise the SS troops on board. They would take over the ship as soon as it was a bit further off shore. They would raise the white flag and would wait for allied vessels.

But the attack by the British planes came about an hour

too soon. The military flag had not yet been removed. The planes bombed the ship. The Cap Arcona sank.

My mother managed to find two other inmates who had survived the camp and the ordeal at sea. Neither knew anything about a planned take-over. Neither had ever met my father. No other inmates or any of the crew members could be located. They had drowned, had been killed near the beach, or had come ashore in the Russian occupied part of Germany. Communication with that part of Germany was not yet possible. We tried to find out whether anyone knew which inmates had been on the Cap Arcona. We had no success. A list of "passengers" that were herded onto the ship did not exist.

However, we established that my father's name was entered into the official concentration camp list of deceased inmates, registered with the familiar date of death: December 27, 1944. Nonetheless, my mother contacted a number of organizations that had been established to locate missing persons. Again and again she received the same condolences: "Unfortunately we have to inform you that your husband died on December 27, 1944, in the Concentration Camp Neuengamme."

Nothing. Always nothing.

●

THE CRACKING OF A WHIP

We lived far enough from center city. Bricks and mortar and not yet driven out nature. All around town it was beautiful. Wild flowers would bloom during spring and summer. Water lilies floated on ponds and in quiet places on the river. Tall trees grew everywhere. From late March to early November our world was lush and green. Only winter brought desolation; yet even then some beauty remained. The many trees, high on the crests of surrounding hills, painted their branches into the pale winter sky.

For a kid, it was nice to live with nature. We could look at it, we could be part of it, and we could use it. I became an "expert" in constructing bows and arrows. A strong hazelnut branch would be flexible enough to bend into a good bow, yet provide enough spring tension to propel my arrows easily more than one hundred yards. Arrows were be constructed from reeds that grew down at the lake. A piece of hollow elderberry branch made an excellent arrow head. Whenever I had a lot of time, I could make an even stronger arrow head by repeatedly rolling the top of the arrow in sand and road tar.

Another tool provided by nature was a whip. True, I did need some string, both for whips and for bows. But string could always be found. To make a whip, I would take a very long piece of hazelnut wood, fasten a string to one end and tie a couple of knots near the loose end of the string. A sharp up and down movement of the whip - and it would crack loudly. Nearly like a pistol shot! Of course, I would never use the whip as a weapon, I only built it to make it crack. I loved to make those sharp popping sounds right behind our house. The "bang" would echo back from the old barn. What fun!

This time I had constructed an especially nice whip. I had found a branch of just the right thickness - not too thin and flexible, but not too heavy and stiff. I carved lines and patterns into the bark of the wood. Yes, this whip turned out to be especially good. It was not only good looking, it worked well! I was proud of it and tried it again and again. Sometimes I would crack it rapidly; at other times I would wait between the "pistol shots" that rang across the space, following after a minute or two with another sharp crack.

Suddenly, I heard rapid steps. Two British soldiers with raised submachine guns stormed into our back yard. Did they look surprised - and just a bit stupefied - when they saw me cracking my whip! They must have thought they had heard real pistol shots!

It was funny. But, on the other hand, I felt just a little odd. But after the two had gone, I started laughing. Now the sound of my whip seemed even more delightful than before.

AN AMERICAN SANDWICH

We tried, again and again, to obtain information about my father's true fate. Had he died in the concentration camp? Had his death been falsified, just to torture us some more? Were they lying when they told us that he had died? Was the statement about his death just a bureaucratic error? Did they possibly tell him that his wife and his child did not want to claim him any longer? He would not have believed it. Had he truly been on the ship <u>Cap Arcona</u>? It would have been just like him to become the leader of the inmates. It would have been just like him to negotiate with the captain. But if he survived the camp, if he truly was on that ship, what had happened to him? Did he drown at sea?

One of the many attempts to obtain more information took us to the city of Schleswig. Another inmate, someone who had been released from the camp before the war ended, yet after my father's supposed date of death, might know some relevant facts, some information that would take us a step forward. My mother wanted to speak with him.

I accompanied her as far as the railroad station in Schleswig. I did not want to talk to that gentleman. I had heard enough horror stories about the camp. I wanted to hear no more. None. It was too horrible, too sad, too depressing. I would wait. So I asked my mother to go by herself. I would meet her at the railroad station later.

I walked through the town and visited the beautiful cathedral. It was pleasant to be in a town that had not been bombed into rubble. Finally I returned to the station to wait for her. It was still two hours before our train would leave. My mother had not yet come back. Probably she would want to spend as much time as possible, exploring whatever she could.

For a while, I walked around the station. The trains were running again. They were now inscribed with "Allied Forces". The insignia of the German Railroad had been removed. Those large inscriptions on the tender of steam locomotives, inscriptions that had read "Wheels must roll for Victory!" were gone as well, painted out with fresh black paint.

154

I was hungry. We still did not have enough to eat. I had eaten breakfast that morning - if one piece of bread could be called breakfast. Now it was nearly four in the afternoon. My stomach was growling.

I sat down in a corner of the train station and watched all kinds of people walking around. Several passengers were crossing the building toward the exit and the city. A train had recently arrived. A few other people were running toward the platform. Probably they wanted to catch that train before it continued on, most likely toward the north, toward Flensburg and Denmark. A few British soldiers were hanging around. I guessed they were waiting for some troop train.

But what was that? That uniform looked different! Maybe it was the kind the two men had been wearing, the soldiers who had stopped at the railroad crossing in our town - on that last day before the occupation. Yes, now I was sure. That soldier must be an American. What was he doing here? I thought this was now a British occupied area?

The American soldier walked very slowly through the station. He seemed relaxed. His gait was hardly military. He saw me sitting in my corner and smiled a bit. He began a wide circle toward the exit. I could watch him well; if he continued on his path, he would walk right past me. And as he was closest to me, he reached into his pocket, pulled something out, and dropped it into my lap. It was a wrapped sandwich! Suddenly, he accelerated his footsteps and was gone.

I removed the paper. What wonderful food! The bread was absolutely white. Nearly like snow. I had never seen anything like it! Between the two slices of bread I found a very thick layer of some kind of meat. I had never seen it before, but it tasted incredibly good.

I would have loved to say "thank you" to that soldier. I could even have said it in English! But he was gone. Well, in that case, the "Thank You" is meant for all those people in the world who help hungry and tired children, wherever they might be.

ORDER TO LEAVE

The British Army was making itself comfortable. Their men needed nice places to live! A lieutenant went from house to house in town to determine which homes in our suburb would be good enough for the soldiers. Ours was. We received an order to vacate our house. We would have two days. Only clothing and a minimum of china could be taken, everything else had to be left behind. The officer made a careful list of furniture, carpets, lamps, vases, utensils and so forth. Everything had to remain in the house. They would check the list when they moved in.

My mother took the train to Kiel to speak with the regional public affairs office of the British occupation forces. She met with the colonel in charge and explained, in fluent English, that our family had been persecuted by the Nazis, that my father had been killed in a concentration camp. She requested that our house would be excepted from confiscation.

The colonel seemed very understanding. He wrote a letter with a strong recommendation to exclude our house from those that would be confiscated. It was not an order, but it was a very emphatic request.

We took the letter to the lieutenant who had ordered us to leave. He read it and laughed. "Fucking nonsense! That's a different command. I don't have to do what he wants. You are vacating your house. By tomorrow!"

What now? All rooms in town were occupied! Fortunately, my best friend's parents offered to help. Their house had a fairly large attic. We could live there! We strung laundry lines from wall to wall, hung blankets over those lines and divided the space. A bed was found. Clothes could be kept in suitcases. At least it was a place where we would survive - until some distant day when we might get our home back. We had no idea whether it would take months or years. But some day.....

It was not to be. Two days later, that British lieutenant felt that his men's living conditions were still too crowded. He wanted more space. This time, my friend's family received the order to vacate. All of us were to be out of the house, again in two days! Once more we had to search for a place to live.

The refugees from East Prussia who had been living in our home, including Mrs. Kipsind and her body lice, had been assigned a room in the old barracks, the place where Italian, Polish and Russian workers had lived during the war. We were to join them. Several families in a single room.

It was a unique experience. At night everyone would be snoring. During the day, people got into each other's way. An old coal stove could not keep us warm. There were no facilities to cook or to wash clothes (no wonder that the Italians had used old tar containers to cook their snails!). During the war, there had been a common kitchen and a mess hall where hundreds of people had been fed. But a refugee minister had received permission to transform the eating facility into a temporary church. Catholic services at eight, Protestant services at ten. The prior kitchen had been divided into more quarters for more families. There was nothing that could be used to heat water or to cook food. Well, we could always eat our beets raw!

A greater problem, however, was the lack of toilets. The POWs who had lived here had shared one toilet among 20 people. We had to share that same toilet with twenty or so families, sometimes families with five or six children! One could only hope that nobody would have an upset stomach!

However, the worst thing about these barracks were the resident bugs. Of course, Mrs. Kipsind continued to threaten us with her body lice. But with some effort we could escape her repeated attacks. Unfortunately, we could not escape the bed bugs that had infested walls and ceilings of the barracks - little flat circular creatures that hid in cracks all day. At night when it was dark, the little brown monsters would emerge and suck themselves round and fat on human blood.

We placed the feet of our beds into cans filled with water. We hoped that this trick would keep them away. But it did not help. The insects would crawl along the ceiling until they had reached a point above the bed. Then they would drop upon us. They preferred my mother to me. She was continuously covered with itching red spots.

The British did not permit us to set foot in our house.

One day, we requested permission to pick up a single electric hot plate. It would have allowed us to cook something in the barracks! The British soldiers who lived in our house had told us that the hot plate was of no use to them. They were fed centrally. Besides, they had our big stove. "Sure you can have it," one of them said when we spoke to him on the street in front of our house. But first we had to get permission from the office.

We tried. The answer was "No!" No Germans were allowed in. And no contents of the house were allowed out. That was the rule. Period.

Despite those harsh restrictions, we soon got to see some of our previous possessions, and we saw them outside of the house! Our beautiful brocade drapes were walking down the street on a rather attractive young lady. She had made friends with the soldiers. The drapery material surely was a reward for her personal services.

This was daily life during the occupation. One day, one of the people in town who had been active in the Nazi party asked me, in a somewhat ironic tone of voice, whether I thought things had become better since the Allied forces had taken over. "Well," I said, "nobody is trying to kill us anymore!"

That is all I said. But I had to admit, at least to myself, that life during the British occupation had not turned out to be as pleasant as I had hoped.

THE SOCK STEALING MACHINE

Life during the occupation was problematic, yet there were some funny moments. One day, a British soldier who had grown up somewhere in the backwoods of England stormed into the barracks. He rushed to confront the people whose house he occupied. Obviously the soldier was quite angry. His face was distorted by outrage.

"Give me back my socks!" he yelled.

The German family was dumfounded. Fortunately, both parents spoke some English. But did they really understand what this soldier wanted? Socks? Why was he talking to them about his socks?

"Excuse me, you mean you lost your socks? But what do we have to do with your socks?"

The soldier was furious. "I want my socks back! Now!"

The German family was frightened. What did he want? What was going on? Was this man crazy? What did he mean with socks? The kind of socks you put on your feet? It did not make sense. "Please explain what you mean," the mother said meekly. "We don't understand."

The soldier yelled, "That German stealing machine took my socks!"

The family was puzzled. A German stealing machine? What was that? The soldier became even more infuriated when they did not respond appropriately. Again, he insisted that he wanted his socks. That stealing machine in the house, in their house, had taken them! He wanted his socks back. Immediately!

Finally, the soldier realized that nobody understood what he wanted.

"Come with me!" he demanded. "I will show you where the socks have gone. In your house. I want you to give them back!"

The father decided to go with the soldier. But he was a bit worried. The occupation troops had ordered us not to set foot inside our houses. Only British troops were allowed to enter. Of course, it was well known that the soldiers invited German girls in. Their lieutenant tolerated it. But would he let an owner come in, despite the strict prohibition?

"You have to come into the house! I don't care what the rules are. You are coming with me, I want my socks back!"

There was no choice.

When they entered the house, the soldier headed directly for the bathroom. "There is that stealing machine. Now give me my socks!"

"But I don't understand! This is the bathroom. Where is the thing you call a stealing machine?"

The soldier pointed to the toilet. Like all German toilets at the time, it was a porcelain bowl filled with water. A wooden seat sat on top of the bowl. A pipe led upwards to the ceiling, ending in a water reservoir. A chain hung from the reservoir. Pulling the chain would send water rushing down the pipe, flushing the contents of the toilet bowl into the drainage pipe.

This British soldier had never seen a flush toilet before. He had grown up with outhouses. The military base where he received brief training prior to being sent to war had not had modern facilities. During the war, of course, the soldiers had used the outdoors. His assigned quarters in our town provided his first experience with a modern toilet. The water filled bowl had looked like a basin, a convenient place to wash his socks.

He had poured soap into the bowl and scrubbed the socks. Of course he could not rinse them in the same soapy water. Fresh clean water was needed. Would pulling on the chain rinse the soap out of the socks? He pulled the chain. Water came rushing down, as he had thought it might. Great! But.... his socks were gone. They had disappeared somewhere down the pipe. Where did they go? To some secret place under the house where those Germans would recover them later? He would not tolerate that!

"I want my socks back!" he insisted again.

The German apologized and tried to explain. There was no way to retrieve the socks. The soldier's socks were gone.

Unfortunately, forever.

A SWIMMING LESSON

The new post-war military government and its German representatives decided to compensate those who had been persecuted by the Nazis. Compensation was called "Wiedergut-machung," best translated as "making up for past wrongs," to make things better again. In a way, it seemed absurd. How could anyone make up for the loss of my father; worse, how could anyone, no matter what they did, create the feeling that things were "good" after all?

But it was a well-intentioned effort. Something was better than nothing. My mother and I received some benefits after we were placed on the list of families that suffered during the Nazi regime. One of those benefits was a paid two week vacation on the Baltic Sea. We were sent to Grömitz, a resort town, not more than forty miles from Kiel. The town's old stately hotels had not been damaged by the war. The town was blessed with a beautiful beach. The nearby shore line was marked by sandy cliffs, not far from the place where the <u>Cap Arcona</u> had been sunk. It was probably one of the places where some of the less weak concentration camp inmates had tried to come ashore. But that was then..

What a different world from the crowded room in the barracks! My mother and I had a room to ourselves! We even had two beds! Outside of our window was the beach and the sound of the waves. It was still summer, warm and lovely. We rented one of the beach baskets - those large, cushioned, two-seaters where one can sit comfortably in the sunshine and dream the hours away. But I did not want to dream! It was time to do things, new things that an eleven-year-old had never done before.

My mother had brought some books for both of us. But I was not interested in reading. The sand and the sea were much too exciting. I walked along the cliffs and collected shells. I watched jellyfish float on the water. I built a sandy fort and defended it against the incessant waves that wanted to do nothing less than destroy my fort, wave by wave, sneakily washing out bits of sand underneath my fortifications until my walls began to collapse.

And, of course, I went swimming. The water was relatively cold, as it always is in the Baltic. But that did not deter me. The sand under my feet was soft and smooth. No stones! I found a place that was shallow enough to walk far out to sea. I could walk to a sandbank about two hundred feet from shore. My hair did not even get wet! A school of fish swam past me. Sea gulls were screaming overhead. It was paradise!

But after a while the cool water had its effect. I was getting cold and decided to get back to shore. For a while I could not find the shallower stretch where I had walked out to reach the sand bank. And I had to find it. True, I said earlier that I had wanted to go swimming, but "swimming" was not quite the accurate word.

Until I was three years old, I had loved water. Every time I saw as much as a puddle, I begged my parents to let me jump in. But then, one day, all that had changed. Strange as it may sound, the reason for my change of mind was milk.

Since we had moved to a suburb of Kiel, we had bought milk from a particular dairy. Farmers brought their milk every morning and the dairy would process the raw milk. The owners would sell milk products, butter and cheese. Until 1937, the dairy had been operated by a Jewish family. It was confiscated by the Nazis and given to one of their own. The new "owner" was greedy - he mixed the milk with dirty water. Several people became ill with dysentery. Seven children were hospitalized. I was one of them. But the nearby hospital was short on staff since all Jewish physicians and nurses had been fired. The remaining employees were overworked. They made errors. A child infected with measles was placed into the room with us. All seven of us became infected. In addition, some of us, including myself, ended up with secondary middle ear infections. Six of the seven children died. I was the only survivor. When I was finally allowed to go home, I was too weak even to walk. For a very long time water had lost all of its fascination.

During the war we could not go swimming. Sure, we could have walked to the nearby lake. But in case of an air attack, we would have been too far away from any protective cover. In other words, this very day in the waves of the Baltic was my first experience with "swimming." To be truthful, I did not know how to swim. I definitely needed to find the shallower pathway toward shore.

I thought I had found it and walked toward the beach as fast as I could when waves crashed over my shoulders. Suddenly, the bottom underneath my feet was gone. Water was above my head. I struggled. For an instant my head emerged above the water and I could breathe. But the next wave covered me again.

What should I do? I had to make a split-second decision. The next time my head came above water I could yell for help. Maybe someone would save me. But - if I did, I would scare my mother to death! I did not want to do that.

"I have to swim!" I concluded. I tried. I had seen people swim. I remembered a couple of movements that I had observed earlier that day when I was watching an older man who was able to stay above the waves. It did not work. I was swallowing salty water. Somehow I remembered another man who had thrown both his arms around in wide circles as he moved rapidly through the water. My mother had called it "butterfly style." I tried it. It worked! I stayed above the surface most of the time. After six or seven wild swings of my arms, my legs hanging motionless below, I could no longer continue. Now I was gasping for air. But I felt sand under my feet! And my head was above water! Saved! My mother never knew!

After coughing some water out of my lungs, I walked slowly and carefully toward the beach, always testing the ground under my next step. I did not want to take the risk of sinking again. Fortunately, I had reached shallower waters. Once at the shoreline, I rested for a while. I did not want my mother to know that I had been in trouble. After I had caught my breath and once my heart had returned to a slower beat, I slowly walked toward our beach basket, dried myself and dressed. My mother looked up for a minute and smiled. She was still reading one of her books. She had not noticed my predicament. I had done it!

I concluded that water was not so scary at all. Now I really wanted to learn how to swim.

That evening I was rewarded for my efforts to conquer

the waves. I have no idea how the hotel did it during this time of scarcity, but they served ice cream! It was incredibly wonderful! I had not eaten ice cream since I was a small child... Yes, this was paradise indeed!

Later, at some other time, in some other place, I did learn to swim well.

A FISHY VACATION

The vacation on the Baltic Sea had begun gloriously. But the next morning, something strange happened. We opened the window and an unfamiliar smell pervaded our room. It smelled like fish, but not quite. It smelled somewhat rotten. We quickly closed the window. After breakfast, we went back to the beach. There was that odor again! What was it? We looked around.

The waves had washed dead fish and other sea creatures ashore. Rotting fish! Had there been a storm? Why were there so many dead fish? After a while we almost became accustomed to the smell and stayed outside. But as the day progressed, the odor got worse. More and more rotting creatures washed ashore. We left early.

The following morning, the stench had become unbearable. The shoreline was covered. Fish. Crabs. Jellyfish. The sea gulls would not touch the rotting dead bodies. They were too far gone.

"What happened?" Most people had no idea. They were just as ignorant as we were. Finally, someone was able to explain all the death at sea. The British forces had destroyed the remaining German ammunition. They could not use Nazi grenades and other explosives: German equipment was metric, theirs was normed in inches. Destroying the ammunition on land was impossible. Finally, they settled on a solution. The ammunition would be detonated underwater, out in the Baltic Sea. The resulting concussion had killed millions and millions of sea creatures. They had been rotting for days. Now the rotting remains of those animals were washing ashore.

We spent the rest of our two weeks far away from the water. At night, we kept all the windows of our hotel room tightly closed. But even without the chance to swim, even if we could not sit in our rented beach basket, the vacation was worth it. I read the books my mother had brought. I found some other boys of my age. Together we explored the inland forests. Going to bed at night was pleasant; we had a room all to ourselves. There were no bedbugs. We still had two beds. It was nice, even if some of that awful smell would drift into the room. Possibly the best part of this vacation, however, was the incredibly wonderful food that we ate every day, except for one evening when the chef decided to serve fish. I could eat only the noodles. Of course, I happily consumed the dessert; that day it was pudding. But fish..... As a matter of fact, I have never again eaten anything that tasted the least bit fishy.

PRISON

Friedrich-Karl's father was a dentist. When the British confiscated their house, he had to vacate the office space in their home. Fortunately for his patients, a tiny room in another house was found to serve as a temporary dental office. A corner of an old warehouse near the railroad track was turned into a lab where X-rays could be developed and false teeth could be constructed. After all, people got toothaches even during the British occupation! Of course, it was not permissible to have a toothache or, for that matter, to get sick after ten PM. The British had imposed a curfew. Anybody caught outdoors after ten PM would be arrested and imprisoned.

One afternoon, a patient badly needed a new set of false teeth. They had to be ready by the next morning. Friedrich-Karl's father went to work in his "lab." He had told his wife that he would be home a little later than normally. They agreed that dinner, if it could be called that, would be delayed until around eight o'clock.

He was not back by eight. Or by nine. Finally it was ten PM and time for the curfew. Still nothing. His wife was worried. But there was nothing she could do; the curfew was absolute.

When her husband did not come home the next morning, Friedrich-Karl's mother became frantic. She went to the lab. Obviously he had worked there yesterday. But there was no sign of him this morning. His temporary office was empty. She went to the English command office in town. But the English soldier on duty only shook his head and waved her away. He did not understand a word of German. She could not communicate in English.

Friedrich-Karl's mother hurried to find a relative who was now employed by the British in downtown Kiel. Fortunately, that lady had not yet left for work. Together, they returned to the local command office. The relative explained the problem in English.

"Sure," answered the soldier. "He is in jail. He was caught crossing the street after curfew. We will keep him in there for a few weeks, at least for a few days. The lieutenant will

167

decide how long."

It turned out that Friedrich-Karl's father had finished the false teeth on the previous night. He had been tired. All he wanted was to have some dinner and go to sleep. He would have to get up early in the morning to fit the teeth. As he finished his work, his clock read twenty minutes before ten. He was crossing the street on his way home when a British soldier stopped him. "You are under arrest for violating the curfew!"

Fortunately, intervention by the relative at a higher level of the British forces set Friedrich-Karl's father free. But the local lieutenant was angry about the interference. That very afternoon, that officer and several of his men spent an hour searching through everything in the dental offices and in the temporary quarters where Friedrich-Karl now lived. Nothing incriminating was found. But several small items, some of them valuable, disappeared with the soldiers.

IN RUSSIAN CAPTIVITY?

One day in the late fall of 1945, a stranger visited us in the barracks. He brought a small piece of paper. Someone in Russia had given it to him. The stranger had been a Prisoner of War in Russia. Only very recently had he been released to return home. When any among the prisoners were allowed to leave for Germany, others would hand them small notes to deliver to their loved ones. Such notes were the only signs of life! The Russians did not permit letters. Sometimes the Russian guards would not notice or would tolerate the crumpled messages. This particular piece of paper was addressed to my mother.

Supposedly, it was a note from my father. The returning POW did not know the man who gave him the note. He could not answer my mother's urgent questions. He was only delivering the piece of paper he had been asked to deliver. That was all.

But how could my father have become a prisoner of war, held somewhere in Siberia? If he had indeed been on the <u>Cap Arcona</u>, if he had been saved by a fishing boat that returned to the Russian occupied part of Germany, if the Russians had thought he might have been a soldier - then it might have been possible. It seemed unlikely, but with some desparate stretch of the imagination, it was possible.

The note began with the familiar but rare words that my parents had always used to address each other. But the handwriting was not quite right. The shape of the letters was similar, yet still somewhat different. Was it a note from my father? Had the stress changed his writing style? Had his hand been injured? With his injuries from the First World War, after a year in a concentration camp, after the attack on that ship, after captivity in Siberia, could he be alive? Could he have survived all that? But why would someone else write to my mother? How would anyone know the terms of endearment they used? Why would another person claim my father's identity?

The note asked for help. My mother did everything to determine whether it was genuine. She contacted the Russian Red Cross and the Soviet government. She questioned returned POWs.

The Russians responded two months later. "Njet! There is no August Streufert in Soviet captivity." All other attempts to determine the accuracy of the note or to find the person who wrote the message failed as well. Returnees from Siberia had never heard of my father. No more notes arrived. Again and again she was told: We are very sorry, your husband died in the concentration camp.

Nothing. Again, nothing.

A DOOR AND A SAIL

Winter. It had been freezing for several days. The water of the nearby lake had turned to ice. Snow covered the roads.

The occupants of a British armored car had tied a sled to the back of their vehicle. The soldiers were pulling German kids around town. A bunch of younger children in the neighborhood each got a turn. They loved it. The soldiers seemed to enjoy it too.

Three of us older boys decided to build a sailing sled. We had heard of such things and we had found a solid door on a pile of rubble near one of the bombed-out houses. That would be the base. Someone brought a broom stick. We centered the stick at one end of the door. It would be our mast. Herbert's mother made a sail from torn clothes. I brought my pair of ice skates. They were fastened on one side of the door, below the edge where the mast had been placed. Gerhard knew where to find another single ice skate. The second of that pair had been lost or broken. We brought all of the parts to Mr. Jansen and asked for help.

The old gentleman was very willing to assist us. He told us that he was quite familiar with our project. Apparently children had built ice sleds when he was a kid. Mr. Jansen drilled a wide hole through our door, centered on the opposite side from the mast. He hollowed out the blade of the single skate, fastened it to a round peg and pulled the peg through the hole he had just made. It fit exactly, allowing us to turn the skate to the right and left. Then he fastened a horizontal piece of wood to the peg where it extended above the surface of the door. It would be the handle for our skate-rudder. We would be able to turn the single skate in back of our sled whenever we wanted to change directions. Finished!

We took our ice sled down to the lake. All three of us sat on the door. I was in the middle, operating the sail. Gerhard, in back, was steering with the rudder. Herbert sat way in front, he would just be a passenger.

What speed! The wind caught the sail and we raced off - turning in wide circles over the lake. But Gerhard was getting a bit too daring.

"Don't steer us so close to shore!" I reminded him. "At this speed we can't stop in time. And you know that we can't make sharp turns!"

"Yea," Herbert added. "You don't have to get crazy!" But Gerhard was not listening. Maybe he did not want to listen. He had always been a bit too carefree in everything he did. On the next approach toward shore he started turning away too late. I dropped the sail. But our sled raced on, heading in a wide circle toward rocks and trees.

"Jump off!" Herbert cried. I flung myself onto the ice. I noticed Herbert close by, sliding across the ice in the same direction. Gerhard was still sitting on the sled, now far ahead of us. Fortunately, the friction of our clothes on the ice was slowing us down. We saw Gerhard finally jump off. Not much later the sled crashed into a rock on the shore. The mast broke. The old door split in two.

Our forward movement slowed. Both Herbert and I stopped comfortably before reaching the rocks. But Gerhard had jumped off too late. He was still sliding forward on the ice when his leg crashed into a tree, right at the edge of land and water.

He limped ashore. "That hurts!" The two of us felt like saying, "It is your own fault!" But neither of us said anything. We guessed that he knew.

DENAZIFICATION

In Nürnberg, the trials of the Nazi leaders were proceeding. Even the less important party members would not get away without some investigation. They would be categorized according to their actions and roles during the "Third Reich." Most of them had been harmless. Some had only joined the Nazi party to be allowed to continue in their profession. Others had thought that party membership might gain them certain advantages. Most had contributed little or nothing at all to the horror which the Nazis had spread throughout Germany and Europe. These people would be "denazified." In other words, they would be free to pursue a normal life. They would become full citizens of a new Germany without restrictions on any political activity.

Others who had actively and intentionally injured their fellow man would be classified according to their former actions. Some might go to jail. Others would get probation but would never again hold public office.

Several prior Nazis from our suburb were under investigation. A few had good reason to be afraid. Among them was Mr. Balser who had been the last Nazi leader in town. Another Nazi party member, Mr. Kamp, had told us that Balser had written an unfavorable report about my father. Since he had come to us with this information immediately after Hitler's regime had collapsed, Mr. Kamp probably thought that his comment would help him in case he himself should ever be accused of party activities.

When the case against Mr. Balser began, my mother was called as a witness. She requested that Mr. Kamp be called as well. However, by now it had become rather evident that the court would be lenient. And, in addition, Mr. Kamp had already gone through the court procedure. He had already been "denazified." No evidence against him had emerged. He had nothing to fear.

My mother testified about the arrest of my father. She revealed that the local party leader had been asked to write a report. She repeated what Mr. Kamp had said: The report written by Mr. Balser had been negative. My father was not released. He died in the concentration camp.

Kamp was called as a witness to support my mother's statement about Balser's unfavorable report. He shook his head.

"Mrs. Streufert," he said, "because of your quite reasonable state of anxiety at that time, you probably misunderstood what I told you!"

There was no proof of misdeeds by Balser. The case was dropped. He, too, was "denazified."

A few years later, Balser tried to run for mayor of our suburb. There was an uproar. People drew little swastikas on posters that advertised his name. He lost the election.

BIRTHDAY APPLES

Yes, the war was over. But food was still very scarce. We could buy only whatever ration our stamps allowed. And many of the stamps were worth only as much as the paper on which they were printed. If a stamp entitled us to a pound of flour, but none of the stores had been able to obtain flour, what was there to do? The ration stamp was worthless.

In the past, the Nazis had always assured us that we were still getting enough to eat. Every month we were told how many thousand units of vitamins had been distributed to each person. The Allies used a different method of persuasion. They did not talk of vitamins. They spoke of calories. "During this month you are receiving eight hundred forty-five calories per day!" It made little difference to us. We were hungry either way.

We laughed about all the propaganda. "They used to feed us vitamins. Now they are feeding us calories. When will they give us something to eat?"

We continued to be hungry. But there were days that counted as exceptions, especially kids' birthdays. A birthday invitation was always a great occasion. Usually, parents saved up whatever foodstuffs they could to make their child's birthday celebration a very special occasion.

I was invited to Theo's birthday party. He was permitted to invite no more than three friends, otherwise there would not have been enough food. Of course I went. We played some games, talked a while and took a walk along the river. But then it was time to eat! Theo's mother had baked a small cake that was quickly gone. I don't remember what kind of cake it was. But the apples that she served after the cake - they remain very distinct in my memory. Five wonderful, polished, red apples!

I could not remember ever having seen such beautiful apples. Sure, during the war a few apples had been available. After all, we lived in a town with many gardens and many apple trees. The families in our town would frequently share their limited wealth. We would give away some of our strawberries; our neighbors would present us with a basket of apples or plums. But all those apples in our town had been various shades of green.

175

These were bright red! And the best thing of all was that each of us could pick out the one that we wanted most. Theo passed the full plate of apples to his three guests.

One apple was especially large. All of us would have loved to eat that one, but we had been taught manners. You just would not take the biggest. Each of the invited kids took a small apple. Theo had known quite well that we would spare the largest one; he wanted it for himself. Before he passed the plate to his younger brother, he took the biggest apple. Apparently Theo felt that his brother could not be trusted to follow the rules of polite manners.

We ate our apples. The taste was fabulous. Actually, in retrospect, I cannot say for sure that these apples tasted better than the green ones we had known. Maybe it was just the unusual bright red color that made the taste seem special.

Theo waited until all of us had just about finished. I had even eaten the core: it was too good to waste. Now he was ready to start on his huge, shiny, red birthday fruit. Probably he intended to make us feel badly. We would have nothing left, but he would still be eating. Theo was that kind of kid.

He could wait no longer. He took a large bite. His face suddenly turned into a grimace. His giant apple had indeed looked large and wonderful on the outside. But on the inside it was completely rotten.

Happy Birthday, Theo!

CIGARETTES

Food was scarce. Cigarettes were completely unavailable. Germany did not grow tobacco. The Reichsmark currency that had been valid during the Nazi time had not yet been replaced. German money was not worth anything. No country would export tobacco to Germany in exchange for our "Reichsmark" money.

The scarcity of tobacco products was hardly new. Cigarettes, cigars, and pipe tobacco had become increasingly scarce during the war. My father had enjoyed smoking a pipe. He would save his tobacco rations for nearly a year, smoke "normally" for a couple of weeks, and would once again stop for about another year.

After the war was over, tobacco was available only on the black market. Every gram of tobacco had become extremely valuable. Smokers picked up cigarette butts whenever they could find them. They would salvage the unburned tobacco, combining the contents of several butts to make a new cigarette. Sometimes we would be captivated by the strange behavior of people who were especially dependent on their nicotine. They would walk closely behind Allied soldiers just to pick up the remnants of a cigarette that a soldier might discard.

It seemed to us that smoking must be something quite wonderful! Otherwise people would hardly go to such extreme efforts to get a little bit of tobacco! I had never tried to smoke. I never had the opportunity. Neither had my best friend. And he wanted to try smoking. But how could we obtain a cigarette? We had no idea. Well, maybe we could make our own!

Behind the garage near one side of Friedrich-Karl's now British-occupied house, there were several trees. The dry leaves from last summer were still on the ground. I believe that they were beech leaves, but I am not entirely sure. We crushed the dry brown leaves very carefully. Once they were crumpled, they fell apart and looked just like tobacco.

Now we needed paper for the cigarette. We found a page from a newspaper. We packed the "tobacco" tightly into the rolled newspaper. Then a match - I had brought a match in my pocket.

Friedrich-Karl lit the cigarette and inhaled. His face looked a bit funny at first, but he was brave and tried a second time. Now he became pale. He started to cough like mad. Then he threw up. It looked awful! Just seeing his agony made me feel as though I would have to throw up too. And his coughing just would not stop!

It was the last cigarette either one of us ever smoked.

RETURN TO NORMALCY?

BACK TO SCHOOL

A year after the war had ended, schools reopened. Friedrich-Karl and I would be sixth graders at the Max Planck "Gymnasium" in Kiel. Only a few of the old building's classrooms were in use; most had been destroyed by bombs. To make room for all of the kids, school was held in two sessions each day. Friedrich-Karl and I had to be in school at eight in the morning. We could go home in the afternoon. Other kids were scheduled for the afternoon session and stayed into the evening. Students from both sessions were to be at the school yard between one and two in the afternoon. At that time, we were served lunch - a bowl of soup. Somebody in some government in some other country must have concluded that it would be easier for German kids to become more reasonable adults than their predecessors if they were able to learn their lessons on a fuller stomach!

On most days, one ladle of watery soup was poured into the containers we brought to school. The soup was usually made of water, vegetables and a few small bits of bright red meat. We called the red bits hedgehog meat. I am sure that it could not have been made from hedgehogs. There were not enough of those cute little creatures in all of Germany to prepare our soup, despite the minimal amount of meat in every bowl. More likely, someone, somewhere, had slaughtered horses to provide all of us with just a little bit of protein. We were grateful.

School at that time was not like anything you would imagine. Of course, we had to learn. There were lessons in German and English, in math and biology, geography and more. There was also physical education, which meant picking up bricks from the rubble and stacking them neatly. Someday those bricks could be used to build new classrooms.

Each of us had to bring one piece of coal to school on every winter day. It was a requirement. If we did not have any coals at home; well, it was up to us to figure out how we could get some. Somehow. A few of the kids told of nighttime raids of railroad cars that were loaded with coal.

The destruction of the school building offered some

180

advantages. The bathrooms for our school were some 800 feet away, in a different building. Toilets in the old school building no longer existed. They had been covered by rubble. We thought of the distance to the bathrooms as a "good thing." The walk to the bathroom and back took several minutes. The time length was especially convenient when we had not done our homework. We knew our teachers. We knew what they did and how they acted just before they would start to ask questions about our last assignment. Just then some of us would request permission to go to the toilet. "I am sorry, but I really need to!"

It had been nice not to have to go to school for a whole year. The fact that the schools had opened again had some advantages and some disadvantages. Most of the time, classes were fairly routine. Occasionally, however, there were moments of excitement. One day, for example, four British military policemen grabbed one of our teachers right in the classroom and marched him off. Why? Nobody would tell us. We never saw that teacher again.

Our relationships with teachers, as one might expect, varied considerably. There was Dr. Palitzky, a gentleman and former professor, who taught art. And there was a Dr. Bornhold, our music teacher. Both were nice and cooperative - generally appreciated by the students. For several years we were taught the various sciences by Dr. Grabowsky, who was tough but fair. But then there was Dr. Meyer, the English teacher. He was our problem.

All of us were very aware that the Nazi period was over. Life as a student under the "command" of a Nazi teacher had not been pleasant. We were not going to tolerate anything that smacked of the authoritarianism which had been rampant under Nazi rule. We were not going to accept another controlling, dogmatic teacher. Specifically, we were not going to tolerate the authoritarian attitude of Dr. Meyer. We found it abhorrent.

Our class had elected a speaker. He talked to Dr. Meyer and told him how we felt.

The teacher just laughed. "I am the teacher. You will do exactly what I want you to do!"

We held a strategy session after school and tried to figure

out how to get to him, without getting into trouble ourselves.

When the next English class came around, we were ready. Dr. Meyer always started every class by pointing to one or another of the students. He would ask specific questions about the reading assignments we had to do after school. Once a question had been answered, Meyer would continue with the next student, and the next one, until all of us had been questioned.

On this rare occasion, all of us had read the assigned texts. All of us would know the answer to any questions he might ask, just in case.

When the first question came, everyone of us raised our hands, volunteering to respond. The student he selected first said, "Excuse me, may I go to the bathroom?"

The answer was an emphatic "No!" He called on the next person.

"I am sorry, Sir, my text had that page missing."

Again he pointed at one of us. "You!"

"The sun is glaring where I am sitting, do you mind if I sit in that seat over there?"

Dr. Meyer was getting upset, possibly even a bit confused. Some of us tried to stifle a laugh. It went on and on. Everyone was responding to his questions with some comment or request that was absolutely irrelevant.

After a while, Dr. Meyer was furious. He yelled at individual students. He screamed at the entire class. His ranting had no effect. We continued our game. Finally he had had too much. He stormed out of the classroom. We applauded. But he was back two minutes later with the principal.

"I want you to see what they are doing!" The principal stood in front, watching carefully. Meyer asked another question. All hands went up. He pointed to a student. The instant response was the correct answer. For five minutes, he fired questions at us. All questions were answered - immediately and correctly.

The principal shrugged his shoulders and left. The moment he was out of the door, we began the game all over again. Irrelevance after irrelevance. And we continued it for three more days. At the end of class on the fourth day, the

182

teacher asked our speaker to stay after class.

"Tell me what you want," he inquired in a subdued tone. A long discussion ensued. Our speaker made it clear that we did want to learn English, but that democratic principles should not only apply to politics but also to relationships among people. The classroom should not be an exception! The teacher agreed to try. And try he did. In fact, after another year or so, we had become pretty good friends with him.

THE PERILS OF TRAVEL

To get to school and to eat some of that lunchtime soup, it was necessary to travel downtown. Getting there was not always easy. But it was usually easier to travel into the city than to return home. Public transportation was still limited. Too many buses, too many train engines and railroad cars had been destroyed during the war. Others, vehicles and trains, were now reserved for the sole use of the occupation forces.

Each morning, a single long train stopped in our suburb on its way downtown. Often it arrived late. We did not mind. Upon arrival we would go to a special counter of the main station in Kiel where a railroad employee would issue a preprinted excuse. "To whom it may concern: This morning's train from Lübeck, scheduled to be at the main station in Kiel at 7:23, arrived exactly __ minutes late." All he needed to do is fill in the number 84 or whatever the exact delay had been. He would initial the slip of paper and hand it to us.

The teachers would accept the official railroad excuse. Fortunately, the first lesson every morning was Latin. We were very glad to miss it, especially whenever the teacher had announced an examination. In fact, we often hoped that the train would be late again. Of course, we would always arrive at school in time for soup at lunch!

Going back home was a different matter. Afternoon trains would not run for yet another year or two. The first scheduled train would leave the main station about five-thirty in the afternoon. By that time everyone who worked in the city would be on their way home. The afternoon train was always incredibly crowded. Passengers arriving during the last five minutes could not even get into the cars. No pushing and shoving would do the job.

Passenger cars on trains of that period were already fifty years old. They were remnants of the Pre-World War I Royal Prussian Railroad. Many doors on the outside of each car led to separate compartments. Some of the cars had little raised platforms with steps leading up to an old brakeman's cabin that was no longer needed, yet the brake wheels in those cabins were still operational. Occasionally, we would find a cabin that was not locked. Sure, it was against the rules to ride up there. But who cared? People were hanging on the outside of the train when they could not push their way inside, and that was even more against the rules - and much more dangerous! Generally, if we did not make an issue of riding in a brakeman's cabin, the railroad crew would look the other way. They understood our predicament. They knew we would not turn the brake wheel to stop the train! After all, it was late and we wanted to go home. The railroad crews knew perfectly well that riding in those cabins, aside from being fun, would be much safer for us than hanging on the outside of the cars.

I would not have hung on outside. A classmate of mine had tried it on a streetcar in the city. At one of the stops, he was knocked off the streetcar by a truck, thrown onto the pavement and run over. He died immediately.

Waiting all afternoon for the train was less than enjoyable. Whenever possible, we would try to get home some other way. For a while, there was a school bus that would take us a good part of the way. But the bus was old and tired. Its motor was noisy and coughed a lot. One winter day, the bus did not come. The motor had failed. It could no longer be repaired. Again, we had to rely on the train or on our own ingenuity.

There was another bus. It took people to the Baltic coast right through our suburban town. The driver had been instructed not to let anyone get off at the bus station in our town. Most of the time, the bus would not even stop. If, occasionally, someone was waiting to get in, someone who needed to travel to the shore, stopping was permitted. But nobody was allowed to ride from downtown to our suburb. We had no idea who had made this rule. It seemed entirely silly to us. There was no competitive transportation. Nobody knew why the rule existed. The bus conductor could not tell us the source of the stupid rule either. Sometimes he would make an exception for us, especially on rainy days; in other words, when the two of us looked particularly miserable.

One day as the bus was about to leave downtown Kiel for the coast, there was enough room for additional passengers. On

that day, the bus actually consisted of something like two buses -
the normal bus with its engine and driver in front was coupled to
what had once been another bus. The attached second vehicle
had been modified; only the passenger section of the old bus was
left. The engine compartment had been cut off, and the driver's
seat, steering wheel, controls and dials were gone. The front
wheels of the old vehicle had been moved a bit to the rear. A
pole had been attached to connect the two buses to each other.
The second bus now functioned as a trailer; it effectively doubled
seating capacity. The conductor in back decided that there
would be enough room for us; Friedrich-Karl and I got a seat in
the rear section.

A cord in the trailer operated a buzzer that the driver in
the front bus would hear. The conductor could pull the cord to
signal the driver in the front vehicle that he should stop.

As we approached the bus stop in our suburb, it became
evident that nobody was waiting to get on. Without a signal, the
bus would continue. The conductor pulled on the cord. But we
kept moving. Again and again he tried. Nothing. Now the bus
turned north onto the road that led toward the shore. We were
speeding downhill. Again the conductor pulled the cord. The
speed was increasing. Was the signal cord defective? Was the
switch broken? Was the buzzer not working? Did the driver
decide to follow the rules, no matter what? Was he refusing to
stop?

What should we do? If we continued all the way to the
shore, we would be stuck. There would be no way to get home
the same day. Our parents would worry, especially after the
evening train had arrived! We did not know anybody at the
shore. We did not even have the money to make a phone call!

"Well," the conductor suggested, "I have an idea. Once
we cross the river, the bus will have to go uphill. It will slow
down. It is full of people and this attached old bus is heavy too.
After a while we will move much more slowly. The old motor in
front isn't that good any more either. That should help. As
soon as we slow down, I will open the door and you can jump
out. What do you think?"

It seemed the only solution! To make sure, the conductor tried one more pull on the cord. Nothing. We would have to jump off on the hill.

We crossed the river at high speed. The driver had accelerated down hill as much as he could to keep from slowing down when the bus climbed the hill beyond the river. Now he had reached the upgrade. The speed decreased a bit, but we were still going rather fast. Now we were already half way up the hill. Then the driver was forced to shift down. We slowed some more. And a bit more. But we were still moving at about fifteen miles an hour and had just about reached the crest of the hill. The other passengers looked at us, wondering what would happen. Nobody spoke.

The conductor pulled the door wide open. I jumped and fell. The briefcase with school materials slid along the road and spilled its contents. My leg hurt, but not badly. Then Friedrich-Karl jumped out. He came down hard on the asphalt. His arm was bleeding. The bus continued, disappearing after it passed the crest of the hill.

"Next time, let's hitchhike!" I suggested.

187

PTSD

I had never been devoted to school. I rarely did my homework. I was bright enough to get by without it - most of the time. And while I did well in the subjects I enjoyed, especially the sciences and in music, I did poorly in subjects that I considered useless. To me, Latin was a complete waste of time. I did not see any point in learning a dead language, one that nobody spoke anymore. English was fun. I would gladly have also learned French or some other living language. But not that stupid, classical Latin! As a consequence of my poor attitude, I never did well in that subject.

I occasionally got caught not knowing the correct answer. Of course, I had not done the work, so how could I have known? Whenever that happened, the teacher would punish me. Typically, I had to memorize another page from Caesar or Cicero or whatever Latin text we were reading at the time. It made me hate that old language even more.

In contrast to Latin, I had mixed feelings about math. Most of the time I was marginally interested - and my grades were acceptable. By necessity I had to get passing grades in math. If I had failed both Latin and Math (in my school failing meant getting less than 90% of the answers correct), that is if I had failed two of what they considered "the four most important subjects," I would have been kicked out of Gymnasium. I would have had to attend a lower level school. That I did not want.

We took four math tests during the school year. To pass mathematics, I had to attain that average score of at least 90% on each of the tests. In other words nine out of ten answers to the math problems had to be correct. I had done marginally on the last exam. My score had been 91%, just barely passing. This time I had to do better to bring up the average.

Fortunately, this time the test was not difficult. It required us to solve equations that contained a number of fractions. I quickly calculated all of the solutions. The teacher had designed questions so that each answer, after all the calculations were done, ended up as a whole number divided by itself. Maybe he was trying to give a clue to those among us who got most of the calculations right but had made a mistake on one or two others. By the time I had gotten this far I stopped thinking. I just wrote down answers. Five over five = five. Three over three equals three. And so forth.

I felt quite satisfied. After school, I walked around in the city. The first signs of reconstruction were visible. I watched new motorized equipment that was digging a deep excavation next to the main street. A fence had been built around the construction site, but some nice person had cut windows into the wooden boards marked "Side-walk supervisor's office." It felt good to see this first rebuilding, the very first signs that the city would come back to life. I enjoyed the afternoon. After all, the test I had just taken would give me a 100% score. Surely I would get a good math grade this year. As a consequence, I would not have to care about Latin. Great!

Three days later, the teacher returned our test. I had flunked. Of course I had known that five over five equals one, and so on. I had made the same stupid mistake on all of the problems! The very same stupid mistake! Of course I had known better! Obviously I had not paid attention! The math teacher, who knew quite well that it was always the same mistake, laughed at me. "They are all wrong answers!" he pointed out. "You flunk! Better do very much better on the last test we will have this year!"

It was a horrible day. I told my mother. She was upset, but tried to be comforting. It did not help. I went to walk in the forest. I listened to the birds, and walked and walked. It did not help. Nothing helped. Finally, it was time to go to bed.

I fell asleep quickly. I was exhausted. And then it happened.

I awoke to the sound of planes, many of them, humming above. I sat up as I heard the first bombs falling. The familiar whistling and howling, the loud detonations! Suddenly everything was brightly lit by those awful yellow and red flames. Our house was on fire! I ran to find my mother; she was not in her room. She must be in the basement... But she wasn't. The noise outside got louder and louder. I was so scared! Something exploded next to me, something hit me, but it did not hurt very much. I ran, trying to hide, but the bombs kept following me. They were everywhere! And that awful yellow and red flickering light! Another huge noise....

But then, suddenly, everything was dark again. And quiet. I could not understand. I found myself sitting up in bed. All I could hear now was some insect chirping outside. It was pitch dark. How could all of the fires have gone out so fast?

I realized only slowly that it had been another one of those nightmares. I had had the same nightmare before. It was one of those experiences that people, much later, would call PTSD - Post Traumatic Stress Disorder. Soldiers returning from war reported them. People would re-live stressful experiences over and over again; they would recur as horrendous frightening nightmares. I lived through nightmares most often when I had been stressed during the previous day.

The bombs would come again and again and again. Each time one of those scary dreams had attacked me, I could not sleep for the rest of the night. I knew that the same nightmare would repeat itself over and over again, once I fell asleep. It was better to get up.

Not being able to sleep now was just as it had been years ago! Then I had been afraid to close my eyes. At that time I would see the flames while I was still awake, even before I had gone to sleep! Now the fires and the bombs would attack me after I had drifted off to sleep. Still the feelings, the fears and the horror were very much the same.

Somehow problems and issues that were small in comparison to Nazi persecution and to air attacks regenerated those much greater horrors of the past.

A VISIT FROM OUTER SPACE

The war was over. Most of the city was still rubble. Many houses in our suburb had not been rebuilt. Most factories and offices were not yet functioning. Consumer goods continued to be scarce, if they were available at all. Among the missing consumer goods were toys.

Without toys, kids had to be imaginative. We had to build our own. We invented toys. We made believe that certain items for adults were actually made for kids. That very kind of "make believe" proved most helpful one day.

Somehow, Friedrich-Karl and I had obtained a small hot air balloon. It had a diameter of about two feet. Suspended about 16 inches below the body of the balloon was a small dish that held a solid chemical, something similar to sterno. Most likely it had been a German Army weather balloon. It was no longer needed. That is, it was no longer needed by the now defunct German Army. We certainly could use it!

If we lit the chemical in the dish, would the balloon inflate? Would it climb into the air? How high would it fly? How far? We were not sure whether the British occupation troops would let us play with it - if we had asked. We decided not to ask. We were just going to try our luck!

We agreed to meet late one beautiful evening. There were no clouds in the sky. Stars were everywhere above, but no moon. We walked some distance away from the main road, crossed an area covered with fruit trees, then stopped at a ravine. No one would see us there.

We lit the chemical. It quickly generated heat. The balloon stabilized and took on a circular shape. In the darkness it looked like a sphere of light - so beautiful! After a minute or so, the balloon started to bounce up and down, as though it was not sure whether it wanted to leave us. But then it must have decided to seek the sky. Slowly, at first very slowly, it began to rise. The fire in the dish illuminated our sphere of light. The balloon climbed upward. For a minute, it seemed suspended above the fruit trees. But then it rose, higher and higher. Finally, it must have been caught by a mild breeze. Still rising, it began to drift toward the road that we had left behind. We guessed its height at about 200 to 400 feet. Now everyone would see it! As it crossed the road it began to drift toward the north-east. Our eyes followed the spherical light for a very long time. The luminescent sphere became smaller and smaller, still drifting up and away. Finally, we could no longer distinguish it from the many stars in the distant sky.

It was over. We said "Good Night" and went home.

The next day, as usual, we took the train to school. A few of the other students asked me whether I had seen the flying saucer. A flying saucer?

"Yes, last night, above the suburb where we live! It was already dark!"

Our classmates downtown knew about it too. They had read about it on the front page of that morning's newspaper! Several people who lived in our suburb were supposed to have reported it!

The paper reported that the flying saucer had been spherical and brightly lit. It had floated low above the trees, but later disappeared into the sky, probably to return to outer space. Maybe the creatures in the saucer had come to observe human life. Once their mission was accomplished, they had returned to their own home planet.

I listened to the excited questions of my classmates.

"Well," I said, "I was outside last night. But I did not see a flying saucer."

"Too bad!" My fellow students were disappointed. But I was telling the truth! Friedrich-Karl and I had not seen a flying saucer!

But now we had another reason to enjoy our "toy" from last night. Flying saucers? Afterwards we laughed and laughed.....

HITCHHIKING HOME

We stopped riding the bus to the shore. But there was another chance to get home earlier than with the evening train. We would walk to the outskirts of the downtown area to a point where the various roads leading toward our suburb came together. All cars and trucks traveling in our direction or beyond had to pass this place. There we stood, waving with onr raised hand, as was the hitchhiking custom at the time. Most often someone would give us a ride home.

Whenever both of us were hitchhiking together, it was fun. It did not make much difference how long it took, even if we had to wait an hour or two before someone would pick us up. But to stand there alone was boring. We often did it, nonetheless, whenever only one of us had been in school or when the other had something else to do in town. Sometimes we were lucky and some car or truck would stop during the first five minutes. It seemed as though cars would stop more often for one kid hitchhiker than for two.

Everyone knew that we had good reasons to hitchhike. Drivers understood how difficult it could be to get home. Generally, they were quite happy to have a "necessity permit" for the use of a motorized vehicle. Their delight to have been selected for such a permit may have increased their willingness to help others who were less fortunate.

Gasoline was still strictly rationed. The few people who did have a permit would try to save as much gas as possible; going downhill they often turned off their engines to let the car or truck coast.

Some drivers who gave us a ride would hardly say a word. Others wanted to talk. At times the conversations could be quite interesting. And sometimes we met people who were quite strange!

I especially remember the driver of a grey and green Opel Olympia, a small pre-war vehicle in relatively decent condition. I was hitchhiking alone that day. I was lucky. The little Opel stopped just as I had arrived at our usual place. The driver must have been about thirty-five years old, but, at that time, he seemed like an "old man" to me.

"I am glad to have company!" he smiled. "What is your name?"

"Siegfried," I responded.

"Where are you going?"

"Just to the next suburb, about eight kilometers from here."

"Too bad, it would have been nice to have company longer than that. I am driving a good bit further."

He stopped talking for a minute as a truck got in his way. Then he continued. "My name is Peter, but my friends call me Pit. You can call me Pit."

That seemed strange to me. Normally, I addressed grown ups as Mr. or Mrs. so-and-so. I never called them by their first names. I could not quite figure out why he wanted me to call him by his nickname. I did not respond.

"What do you like to do?" he wanted to know.

What should I tell him? That I was able to play a musical instrument, a zither? That I liked to play with electric trains? Old ones, trains I had gotten for Christmas long before they disappeared from the stores? Or that I liked to read, especially books written by Karl May, those books about the American Indians? I decided that I would talk about the books.

"I read a lot. Karl May books, for example. I just finished one about the Indians in the Llano Estacado."

"Karl May..." He seemed to think out loud. "When I was your age, I read a lot of his books too. Do you know that he wrote several volumes about adventures in the Arab countries?"

"I read a couple of them. But I think the books about the Indians are more fun. Especially those about Winnetou, the Apache chief."

After nodding his head a few times, he added casually, "I still have a few Karl May books at home, in Eutin. Would you like them? I'll give them to you."

The man was getting stranger all the time. People don't just give away books! They are worth a lot, especially at a time when there are none for sale. I must have looked bewildered.

"Yes," he smiled directly at me, "if you come with me to

194

Eutin, I will find those books for you. I think they are on the upper shelf in my bedroom. And later I will drive you back home. How about that?"

Eutin was another thirty miles beyond our suburb. His offers did not make sense. Why would he waste gasoline to drive me back, after giving me books that he should keep? I was getting a bit uncomfortable. Why was he trying to bribe me? Why did he want me to come home with him?

I resisted. "Thanks a lot. I can't come today. My mother is waiting for me." I wanted to get away from this man.

He knew quite well that I was not telling the truth. "Your mother is not waiting for you right now. How can she know when you will get a ride! And if you had taken the train, you would not be home until sometime around six. I promise to get you back by then." He put his arm around my shoulders. The car was small. It was easy. He would have been able to touch the window on the passenger side, without even bending or stretching!

His strange behavior made me more and more uncomfortable. I did not want to be touched. And we were already entering the suburb where I lived.

Suddenly he pulled a picture out of his pocket. "Look at that!" he announced. "Isn't that pretty?" It was the picture of a young girl. Completely nude! Yes, she was very pretty. I had never before seen a picture of a nude girl - except in a medical textbook on my parents' shelf. But those pictures were not of pretty women. Those were diseased people, with growths or red spots all over them. But this picture - it looked very nice. I could not stop looking at it.

Suddenly he took his arm off my shoulders. His hand reached for my lower body. "I have a lot more pictures in Eutin. Even nicer ones than this!" His voice had become very soft. "I will show them all to you. And I will give you all of my Karl May books!"

Now I knew that this was one of the men my mother had spoken about. She had warned me. "Watch out for homosexual men! They can do whatever they want to each other, but don't let them get close to you!"

195

Somehow I had to get out of his car. Would he stop if I insisted? Probably not. After only one more kilometer I would be home.... How could I get out of this situation? How could I get him to stop?

We were not far from the railroad tracks that crossed the road in our town. The gates started to come down. He had no choice, he had to slow down. A freight train was approaching.

The little Opel had not quite come to a stop when I opened the door, grabbed my case and jumped out. "Thank you for the ride!" I called out as I quickly closed the door and ran into the nearest house as though I lived there.

●

THE BOAT

It was a Friday afternoon. Although Herbert, Gerhard and I had arrived relatively early at the train station, there was only one empty seat in a compartment car. Herbert sat down. We had agreed that he could sit - if he would place his briefcase flat on his lap. That briefcase would be the table for a card game we were planning. Not long ago, we had learned to play "Skat." This bidding game helped us to pass the time on the ride home, especially during the last two or three weeks.

They were repairing much of the railroad track between the main station in downtown Kiel and our suburb. The train had to move very, very slowly across the not quite finished sections of brand new tracks. We were not especially happy about the lengthy delays and s-l-o-w motion. A few days earlier, we had been so exasperated that we posted a sign in one of the train cars: "Milking cows or picking flowers prohibited while the train is in motion!" The railroad crew apparently failed to appreciate our humor. The following day our sign was gone.

Nonetheless, the slow progress of the train had one advantage. There was enough time for several rounds of our card games. We never played for money, but we agreed to compete for favors. The winner of the day could ask one or both of the other players for a favor - and as long as the request was somewhat reasonable, the losers had to honor it.

As the train finally approached our suburb, we had already played more than twenty rounds of Skat. All of us had accumulated about the same number of points. The last game would decide the winner! I looked at the cards Gerhard had dealt. They were terrible! But, maybe... In Skat you can bid to lose every trick. I bid to lose, won the bid and placed all of my cards face up on Herbert's briefcase. Both Herbert and Gerhard tried to find some way, some sequence of plays, where I would have to take at least one trick. No luck. All the lowest cards had been in my hands! I had won!

Now it was my chance to ask for a favor. Great! I needed help. I wanted to take my newly built Kayak boat down to the lake. The boat was much too long and too heavy for one person to manage. I asked for help. Gerhard apologized, he could not do it that Friday. His parents had assigned him chores for the evening. But Herbert was willing to cooperate: "Can we ride out into the lake in your new boat? It is a two-seater isn't it? Can we try it? Still tonight?"

"Sure!" After all, I wanted to test the boat as soon as possible!

When I had told them about my "newly built" boat I did not quite tell the truth. "Rebuilt" would have been a better word. A few months earlier, I had seen the skeleton of an old Kayak in a neighbor's yard. I asked whether it might be for sale.

"You can have it." The neighbor shook his greying head. "There is no need to pay for it. It is probably of no use. I'd be glad just to get it out of here." Of course I took it.

But the boat I had so easily acquired was just a skeleton of narrow wooded slats, woven in a criss-cross pattern into the general shape of a "Faltboat." A Faltboat is similar to a kayak, about 20 feet long and maybe two feet wide. Two seats in the very center are placed directly behind each other. Once upon a time, a rubberized skin must have covered the now empty slats of this kayak skeleton - except, of course, in the very center where the seats had been placed. Without its skin that kayak would not float. I would have to get a new skin for my boat! Of course, there were no skins to be had in any of the stores. What could I do? Somehow I had to make one! Somehow I would manage....

I found a few old sheets. All of them were worn with holes here and there. Of course, those badly damaged sections of cloth would have to be cut off. I would also need a large quantity of rubber cement. The flexible cement would let me glue the various pieces of sheet into a single skin and would make the boat waterproof. I inquired in local stores and factories. One stationary store was able to sell me a small tube of rubber glue. The clerk laughed when I asked for a large can. "I haven't seen that much since before the war! You can forget that one!" The tube he offered would not help. It was much too little. But then I found a furniture manufacturer that used rubber cement to glue cloth from unused German Air Force parachutes onto plywood boards. Yes, they could sell me some!

I was quite proud of my smelly treasure. Now I would finish my boat! The salvageable parts of the old sheets were cut to size and glued to each other. Then they were stretched and glued to the wooden slats to create a watertight kayak. Now it looked right! Only the very center portion with the two seats was left open.

I painted the entire skin of my boat with the remaining rubber cement. I wanted to ensure that water would not filter through the material. I even found a can of red enamel paint. It was not quite the right material for a somewhat flexible kayak, but it would have to do. Once the rubber cement had dried, I colored the boat a bright red. If I could have obtained a little paint in some contrasting color, I would have given the boat a name - but after the rubber cement and the red paint my luck ran out. There was nothing else available. No matter, some day my boat would surely have a name, even if it would have to wait. No, even if "she" would have to wait a while. I would not call my boat an "it." Someone who knew all about boats told me that boats are always female. Calling a boat an "it" would bring bad luck and bad luck I did not need.

My kayak was finished. She was ready for her element. Today! After winning at Skat, Herbert would have to help me carry her down to the lake!

It was a long walk with the long, heavy boat on our shoulders. Part of the path was uneven, pitted with potholes and covered with rocks. Walking those two miles took nearly an hour! Again and again we set the boat down. Even though we were mostly walking downhill, we were forced to rest from time to time. But finally we reached the lake.

After bouncing on our shoulders for all that time, my boat had begun to sag in the middle. New kayaks are held together tightly. Their skins consist of several layers of woven material - interspersed with several sheets of rubber. That greater thickness and the tight stretch of the material lends them the needed stiffness. A skin like that would have made my boat much stiffer as well! But my single layer of old sheets painted with rubber cement was much too weak. The middle of the boat

sagged seriously. But at least the skin had not torn on our way
down to the lake. Sure, I would have to be careful with my new
kayak - but as long as it floated -that would be just fine.

We gently placed one end of the boat into the lake and
slowly, carefully pushed it forward until all of it was in the water.

Something was wrong! The boat listed to the left about
20 degrees. I could not imagine why - there was nothing heavier
on one side than on the other! Then I remembered the words of
the gentleman who had freely given me this skeleton. Did he not
say, "It is probably of no use...?"

No! It was going to be of use! I would not let his
pessimism deter me! My boat would float proudly upright!
There is a solution to everything: both of us would have to sit a
bit more toward the right - that would straighten the boat out!

Herbert climbed in first. The middle of the boat sagged
when he got in, even in the water. Before he got settled, my
boat tilted even more to the left. But he shifted his position and
it listed less. Now I knew it would work! It was my time to
climb in. I would sit in the back seat. That way I could move
the rudder by pushing my right or left foot against the pedals.
The pedals, in turn, were connected with string to the rudder in
back.

I climbed into the seat. It was not difficult. Only my
feet got wet - but that did not matter. The boat moved back and
forth a bit, as though it had been caught in the waves of some
passing speedboat. But there were no other boats nearby. A
rowboat in the distance did not create any waves at all. As I got
in, I could feel the middle section of my kayak drop downward
by another three or four inches. The water was now threatening-
ly close to the top of the boat. But the front and back ends of
the kayak seemed to soar out of the water.

I must have looked doubtful. Herbert noticed my
concern and tried to comfort me. "Good thing we don't have
waves on this lake!" Of course he was right. But I was not only
worried about waves. We would have to be very careful not to
move too much toward one side or the other. If we tilted the
kayak just a little too much, the water would spill into our boat.

We gingerly set off away from the shore. We moved our

paddles through the water and the boat moved forward. It worked! True, my boat still listed a bit to the left, but it did not matter! We were moving! I had my own wonderful boat! It was a boat I had built, no, rebuilt - all by myself!

Suddenly a sharp stone scraped the underside of the rubberized skin. A long gash opened. Water surged into the space where we were sitting. The center of the kayak dropped below the water line. The water of the lake was pouring in. In less than half a minute the boat sunk. Both of us were in the water. Fortunately, we were both good swimmers.

"You mean we carried that thing all the way down here just to get soaking wet?" Herbert complained.

I was not in the mood to listen to complaints after losing my boat. "Well, you did owe me a favor. I could just have told you to jump in the lake. But then you probably would not have done it!"

"You guessed right. Anyway, let's get home and dry off. It is getting dark and a bit cold."

Getting home sounded like a very good idea - even without my boat. But on the way home I promised myself that some day I would have a real Kayak. Not a rebuilt one. And, come to think of it, at least I had not named this one yet. I could save whatever that name would have been for my next boat. Then, maybe, I would have more luck.

Or, did my boat sink because it did not yet have a name? A female name at that?

LATIN TEACHER AND HERO WARRIOR

Our first Latin teacher had been fun, even if I did not like his subject. I remember his first words very well. He entered the classroom of about 30 boys, all at the age they are getting very interested in girls. I still remember his words:

"Imagine. It is evening. The sun has set some time ago, but the full moon is casting shadows of tree branches above. There, in a park, a boy and a girl are sitting on a bench, close to each other. He puts his arm around her. They look deeply into each other's eyes. The world has disappeared for them, they are only aware of each other. What they are thinking, what they are doing is 'amare.' It is a Latin word that means 'to love'. And that word is conjugated as follows:

    amo means I love

    amas means you love

    .....

The next year we were assigned a different teacher and, unfortunately, he stayed with us through the following years. He was of slight build with thinning white hair. He looked very severe, a characteristic that was emphasized by his wire rim glasses. To him, Latin was the most important thing in the world. In his view, anyone who did not understand or appreciate the old language was barbaric, uneducated, and, in effect, worthless. His rigid authoritarian and dogmatic demeanor made him quite unattractive to his students.

I had never liked Latin. Now I hated it even more. And my obvious dislike for his favorite subject was something he did not appreciate. In turn, I did not appreciate him. I rarely did my homework. I did not practice vocabulary. I remembered most of what I heard in class and just tried to get by.

Some of the other kids would cheat whenever we had a Latin test. Tiny translations of all Latin texts could be bought in book stores; they were small enough to be conceiled in your hand. They passed their tests by copying whatever the miniature book said. I never owned such a little book. Instead, I usually thought up some excuse when I did not have the correct answer. It worked for me. Unfortunately, the kid sitting directly behind me was not quite as verbally facile as I was - so he was repeatedly scolded by the teacher.

One day when the teacher demanded answers to a very difficult question, the kid behind me just stuttered a few incoherent words. His face turned bright red. The teacher came running from the front of the classroom and stood right beside me as he grabbed the student's clothes and pulled him upwards. Then he bent forward until his face was no more than three inches from my neighbor's nose. He screamed at him: "If I were still a major, I would have you shot!"

All of us were shocked! We had thought that such Nazi behavior was a thing of the past!

About two years later something quite funny happened. The same student, sitting in the same seat behind me, was again unable to answer the same Latin teacher's question. Again the teacher stormed forward toward the student. Again he was standing right next to me, ready to attack the young man in the seat behind me. Again he started screaming: "If I were still a major......"

This time the guy behind me did not have to be pulled up by his clothes. He had grown quite a few inches. He got up all by himself. Very slowly. By the time the teacher yelled the word "major" his head was already at the same level as that of the teacher. But the student was still getting taller. Not only taller; he was big, he had become an excellent soccer player with huge muscles.

The teacher took two steps backwards. The student was still slowly rising, now already a foot taller than the teacher. And the "major" never finished that familiar sentence. He looked surprised, shocked, shook his head, backed up some more, turned and quickly walked back to the front of the classroom. When he started speaking again, it was about a different topic.

This triumph over pedagogical terrorism called for a victory celebration. Our "fearsome" Latin teacher was not a "major" hero after all.

MILITARY POWER FOR THE ERECTOR SET

In addition to my old electric trains, I owned a "Trix" construction system, a kind of erector set. I had enjoyed building all sorts of things over the years, always making sure that no parts would be lost. After all, replacements were not yet available. But by now I was a bit too old to construct equipment that had to be operated with a hand crank. It was time for external power, for an electric motor. But how could I obtain one?

I told an eighteen-year-old from the neighborhood about my needs. "No problem!" he told me. "That's easy."

He asked me to come to his "laboratory" the next evening. The lab turned out to be just a corner of a shack where his family kept gardening supplies. As I arrived, he was busy fastening a small transformer to a wooden board. When that was done, he connected a rectifier to the transformer. Wires led from the rectifier to a terminal that would supply twenty volts DC. Finally, he pulled a small motor from a pile of equipment in cardboard box. "That is for you. It should work just fine for your construction set."

"Great, thank you so much!" I was already thinking of all the machines I would now build, things that I could power with this little motor. I would have liked to start right away, but I needed to ask him one question, just out of curiosity.

"Where do you get all this stuff?" After all, he could not have bought those parts anywhere. The stores were still empty.

"Easy! There are old German mines drifting ashore. I know a place where I can find them from time to time. I take them apart. There are all sorts of useful parts inside! Your motor is one of them!"

CONFIRMATION

For two years, Friedrich-Karl and I had to go to the local "church," once each week in preparation for our confirmation ceremony. Religious services were still held in the semi-sanctuary of the barracks. We were supposed to attend services, and sometimes we did. However, we could not avoid an hour a week on Thursday evening when we had to appear for religious instructions. Two years of attendance was a requirement for confirmation in our church.

Both of my parents had been members of the Lutheran church since birth yet had never been enthusiastic about attending organized religious services. We had never spoken much about the Bible or about organized religion. Nonetheless, both parents had been basically "religious" people - in their own way.

My parents felt that I should have my own choice in matters of religion. To make sure I could exercise that choice, they had arranged for me to be baptized after birth. My mother later argued that I should go through instruction and confirmation, just in case it would ever be important to me. I went.

I don't remember much about those lessons. Other events from those hours of religious instructions seemed more interesting and remain fixed in my mind. One day, the minister showed up tired and obviously stressed. He told us that he had been present during the birth of his first child. He seemed very upset. The birth process had been a terrible ordeal for his wife. He assured us that the two of them would have no more children. Absolutely not.

But they had five more.

And I remember that we kept asking the minister questions that he did not appreciate. For example:

"There is something we don't understand. God created Adam and Eve, right? They had two children, Cain and Abel. Just two. Have we got that right so far? Good. Now, Cain was nasty and killed Abel. And then Cain had kids of his own. True? But with whom? With Eve?"

Or one of us would ask, "Dear Minister, would you be so kind and explain the text of Ezekiel 23?"

205

I don't think he liked either one of us. I am still amazed that he did not kick us out. I am surprised that he did not refuse to confirm us. He should have done exactly what he told us God had done when Adam and Eve ate that apple: "Out with you!" I am sure that he viewed us as "bad" people who would someday go to hell! I am sure we helped to strengthen that impression once he had confirmed us; we never showed up in his church again.

About three years later, both Friedrich-Karl and I had become deeply involved in photography. Both of us had obtained very good 35 millimeter cameras with multiple lenses - something that was still quite rare at the time. We used those cameras frequently, both for landscape photography and to make a bit of money taking pictures at official occasions and parties.

One day, someone told me that the minister wanted to take pictures at a church occasion. However, he did not have a camera. He tried to borrow another person's camera, but that individual had refused. A camera, at that time, was still a highly prized object!

I met the minister a couple of days later as our paths crossed near the local train station. "Good morning," I said. "Someone told me that you need to borrow a good camera."

He looked astonished. "True. But I don't know anyone who would let me borrow one."

"You are wrong, you do know someone! You can borrow mine. Any time."

The astonishment on his face was overwhelming. In a way, it was nearly funny. And a few days later, someone else told me about a conversation that gentleman had with the minister. "I just don't understand Siegfried Streufert!" the minister had wondered. "He was always such a problem when I tried to teach him religion, you know, before confirmation. And he never comes to church. And now he is behaving like a real Christian. But, - - his behavior still is not what you would expect from a Christian. He never comes to church! I simply don't understand it!"

NEW MONEY

We were to get new money. The old currency, left over from the war and the Nazi period, was worthless. The stores had been empty. Little had been available during the last years of the war or during the three years since. The black market was flourishing. People traded their illegal wares right across the street from the main train station in downtown Kiel. Anything could be sold or bought for American dollars. Most of the time, both the Allied and the German police would ignore all that activity. Only occasionally would they make a show of closing the market down. But when the police did intervene, their raid would begin very slowly, allowing most of the traders to get away. All of them would be back an hour or so later.

One of the local boys, somewhat older than I, became a frequent trader on the black market. A middle aged lady in town had seduced him. She used him. She would attend to his sexual needs in return for his willingness to serve as her personal trader at the black market. Apparently she did rather well - and, of course, she never had to take the risk that she might be arrested. Her "slave" spent a couple of days in jail, but he was always willing to go back to her and to the black market.

All that was about to change. With a new currency, the black market would become unnecessary. The new money would be worth something. We would receive one new German Mark for each ten old marks, but only if we could prove that our money had been on deposit for several years. Exchanging only money that had been in the bank for years kept black marketeers, many of whom had amassed millions of old Marks by their illegal trading, from cashing in on their profits.

But what good would it do? True, whatever money my mother had in her accounts was deposited long before the end of the war. But if something that would have cost 100 old marks would now cost 100 new German Marks, we would lose ninety percent of our savings! In effect everything, including food, would now be ten times as expensive! Rents would go up tenfold! The monthly social security payments we received would be reduced to one-tenth of the old amount. In a way it seemed that this money exchange would be equivalent to legalizing the black market! I could not imagine the consequences.

Over the years I had saved some money of my own. After all, kids were encouraged to do that. I was no exception. I now owned about fifty marks. Old marks, of course. In cash. Tomorrow all that money would be worthless. It had not been on deposit in some bank. My money could not be exchanged. I had to spend it. Quickly. But how?

As I was about to leave for school the day before the new money would be issued, I asked my mother what I should buy. Her answer was not very encouraging.

"I don't think you will find much!"

I did not want that to be true. Sure, I knew that the stores had been effectively empty for years. But money is supposed to be a means of exchange. And I had saved for years to accumulate my wealth, my fifty marks!

I had been in the stores. I had not seen anything truly worthwhile. I never saw the electric trains I was looking for. I did not even see toy trains with wind-up motors. Nonetheless, occasionally I discovered something that was not all that bad. Two or three months ago, for example, one of the stores had a wooden train for sale. Printed paper had been glued on top of the wood to make the train look more real. It was supposed to have been the "North Express," a train from Copenhagen to Paris. I had once been near the actual North Express; It was again scheduled through Germany.

On first look that little wooden toy train with the glued on paper had not looked so bad. If I put it somewhere in the back of a train set, and if no one looked at it carefully, it might even have been taken for a real metal toy! Of course, I had not bought it that day. After all, I was supposed to be saving my money rather than spending it! Now I wanted to buy it, or something of that kind. I wanted to find something, anything that I could use as a decoration for my old train set! I wanted to spend all of my fifty Marks. Tomorrow it would be worthless!

When school was over, I walked directly to the toy store where I had seen that wooden train. The store was open for business - but empty. In one corner I discovered a few marbles.

They were made of ugly brown clay. Someone had formed them and probably dried them in their oven at home. Those "marbles" were not even round! They would never move in a straight line!

That was all the store had for sale! What could I possibly do with a few ugly, uneven marbles! I asked the sales clerk. No, he assured me, they had nothing else. Nothing in back of the store either. Sorry!

I visited a few more stores. A number of people were on the same mission. Everyone wanted to get rid of their old money. Everyone wanted to find something useful. Yet other people tried to change their paper currency into coins, believing that coins would not be devalued. Neither of them would be in luck: there was no useful merchandise to be bought anywhere. And as we found out the next day, old coins would be just as worthless as old paper money.

I finally returned to the toy store and bought the ugly brown marbles. I never used them. A year later I threw them out.

The next day, the day of the new money, I went to the same stores. This time I had no money to spend. But I wanted to look. I could hardly believe my eyes when I saw the window of the same toy store, the very store which had been completely empty yesterday. Three different electric Märklin trains were sitting there! Different sizes at that! And hundreds of other toys, anything you could want - anything all of us kids had desired for so many years. Most of the toys in that window were not even expensive. For my fifty marks, if they had been the new kind of Marks, I could have bought an electric train engine, a couple of cars and even some tracks. But I no longer had fifty marks. At least not the new kind.

How could the Märklin company have manufactured the trains in that window during a single night and transported them several hundred miles to Kiel? How could the personnel of the store have received and set up the merchandise in that window, again during that same night, even before the store opened in the morning? After all, the clerk, with a perfectly honest face, had assured me only yesterday that they had absolutely nothing in their inventory!

The world had changed. The new money was here. The three occupation zones in the West of Germany had been united. Were we still Germans or would we be identified as the Three-Zone people? Kiddingly we called ourselves "the natives of Trizonesia." A new German constitution was in the works. Soon the adults would vote for our own government. The British moved out and after more than three years we were able to return to our house. It was a mess: The soldier's dogs had not been housebroken. Persian carpets and upholstered furniture were ruined. There were deep cigarette burns on all the wooden furniture. Lamps were ripped off the ceiling. The drapes were gone. And most smaller items were simply missing. But at least we could move back into our own space. I would have a room to myself!

Life was changing for me as well. I was old enough to fall in love with my first girlfriend. My mother was in treatment for cancer. For the first time since I was a child, we were allowed to travel more than a few miles without obtaining a permit. Some of my friends and I would spend days, riding hundreds of miles on our bicycles to explore our new world.

One thing was sure. It would be a very different world than the one we grew up with. We would see to that!

ABOUT THE AUTHOR

A few people read these tales before they were published. Several among them asked, "And what happened afterwards?" A few words about the author might satisfy that curiosity.

Siegfried Streufert was born in Berlin in 1934. When the German parliament in Berlin was dissolved and the Nazis took over the government, August Streufert, Siegfried's father lost his senatorial seat and his government job. Blackballed by the Nazis, August was unable to find a job for some time. He finally found employment with the Dutch "Van Houten" chocolate and cocoa company. The family relocated to Kiel, a large harbor city on the Baltic Sea, not far from the border with Denmark. There they settled in the suburb of Raisdorf.

Raisdorf offered a measure of security. Many of the people who lived there had worked their way up to "foreman" in the Kiel shipyards. They had bought comfortable but relatively small houses in Raisdorf. Prior to the Nazi take-over most among them had belonged to liberal political parties. Many were still vehemently opposed to the Nazi regime. August Streufert felt safer in such a town - much safer than he would have felt in a more well-to-do (and more conservative) part of the city. The experiences of Siegfried's family in Raisdorf and Kiel are described in this book.

Later, at the age of seventeen, Siegfried Streufert was selected to be an exchange student to the United States. He spent one year in Amarillo, Texas, but returned to live another four years in Germany before settling in the United States. After obtaining Bachelor's and Master's degrees at Southern Methodist University in Dallas, he completed his doctorate at Princeton University. Since that time he has been a professor at Rutgers, Purdue, Bielefeld (Germany) and Pennsylvania State Universities with an interim year as Resident Scholar at the National Institutes of Health in the Washington D.C. area. At present, he is a professor at Pennsylvania State University, College of Medicine, in Hershey, PA.

While Dr. Streufert has published a number of books and some 250 articles, this is his first "popular" book. Everything he wrote previously focused on the sciences to which he has contributed: behavioral medicine, pharmacology, psychology and management.

Dr. Streufert lives with his wife, Dr. Glenda Nogami, in Harrisburg, Pennsylvania.